First published in 2014 by:-

Chris R. Pownall

Spanning a Lifetime – A book about bridges with associated stories.

ISBN – 13: 978-1494291143
ISBN – 10: 1494291142

A catalogue record of this book is available from the British Library.

Disclaimer – All facts presented in this title were gained from common and reputable source in print and on the Internet. If any detail within this title is found to be incorrect, the author will be pleased to be notified.

Spanning a Lifetime

A book about Bridges with associated stories

By

Chris R. Pownall

Table of Contents

ACKNOWLEDGEMENTS

- Anthony Peate – East Cheshire Council, Highways Department. - Re: Penn Bridge Bosley.
- Alistair Steele - Gilbert Gilkes & Gordon Ltd – Re: Water Turbines.
- Basil Jeuda - Re: Macclesfield Canal Bridges.
- David Kitching - Re: Macclesfield Canal Bridges.
- Peter J. Robinson - Re: Foryd Bridge Rhyl.
- James Hall (Uwch Peiriannydd Pontydd) Senior Bridge engineer - Re: Foryd Bridge Rhyl.
- Mr Chick Flack – Re: Makaranga Garden Lodge Hotel, South Africa.
- Mrs Danna Flack – Re: Makaranga Garden Lodge Hotel, South Africa.
- Ryan Coppin – Re: Makaranga Garden Lodge Hotel, South Africa.
- Leon Long - China Highlights Travel Company. Re: Nanpu Bridge Shanghai.
- Eileen Faires - Bridge Watch - Re: Cross Keys Bridge.
- Michael Strietzel - Re: Charles Bridge, Prague.
- Eric C. Bell - Re: Sunshine Skyway Bridge, Florida.

Foreword

I have always appreciated the structure of bridges, be they small or large, and constructed from stone, timber, concrete, iron & steel, aluminium, or a combination of any, or all of these materials.

Not only do I find most bridges very pleasing on the eye, but I admire the architectural and engineering design that goes into building them.

The bridges described in this book are included for various reasons. Some invoke specific memories, whereas others, rate particularly high, within my league table of great bridges. They are all bridges that I have either, crossed over, passed beneath, or simply visited, some close to home, and others from my global travels.

Bridges are amazing structures, and I marvel at how ancient civilisations including the Romans, were capable of designing and constructing bridges from timber and natural stone. Furthermore, how they ever understood the nature of the forces involved, and how these were calculated to provide a bridge capable of spanning a river or a valley, with a functional load bearing capability.

There have been many disasters involving bridges and design and construction engineers have great responsibility to provide structures that are highly functional and safe.

Bridges are symbols of a nation's development, with bigger and longer structures now being constructed in many parts of the world.

I also appreciate fine looking historic ships, so there are a few of those included amongst the bridges, simply for my self-indulgence.

I hope you enjoy reading about the bridges I have selected in this book, for their interest and connection with my journey through life.

1

Penn Bridge - Bosley

This single arch stone bridge, constructed in 1856, is situated very close to the place of my birth in the small village of Bosley, in rural England. There are five domestic dwellings located alongside the bridge, which spans a small river known as Bosley Brook, and I was born at house number three, in the year of 1943.

Penn Bridge supports a local highway named Tunstall Road, and I must have passed over it many thousands of times during the period of my life, when I resided at this location.

The bridge itself invokes fond memories, whenever I relate to it, as I associate it with my childhood and adolescent years, in this picturesque rural locality.

In the summertime, I would sleep with my bedroom window wide open, and the sound of Bosley Brook rippling close by, was a soothing and pleasing sound that I shall always remember.

As a young lad, I would occasionally construct a dam beneath the bridge, using stones piled up across the river, backed up with sods of earth. I guess this was a silly thing to do, but it was great fun, when a wall of stones was holding back a head of water up to two feet high. The real thrill came when I breached the dam, and the escaping rushing water, gave me an appreciation of the available energy from a flowing river.

Whilst Bosley Brook is only a small river, it provided power to a mill approximately half a mile upstream, plus another mill further down river, at the location where it enters the much larger River Dane. I have written separately about the downstream mill in my book entitled 'Dane Mills Bosley'.

When I was a young lad in the 1950s I remember the upstream mill was an ice factory, producing large blocks of ice for local fishmongers, hotels and restaurants. There were no refrigerated vehicles in those days, therefore customers for the ice, had to be within a certain distance from Bosley Village, for obvious reasons.

This mill had previously been a corn grinding mill, powered by a single water wheel, which was also fed from Bosley Brook.

There was a mill pool that created a sufficient head of water to provide the necessary power to drive the machinery.

The mechanical power for the ice making plant was produced by a Gilbert Gilkes & Gordon Ltd 'Francis' type, water turbine. The output shaft was mechanically connected to an ammonia compressor, which circulated the refrigerant within the chilling equipment.

7

The turbine was a 13.5inch series 4 'Francis' type machine, capable of generating 14.4 horse power from a shaft speed of 430 rpm. This required a 25 feet head of water and a flow rate of 180 litres/sec. The serial number of this turbine was 3496 and it was installed in 1928.

I can clearly recall visiting the ice factory and it was an impressive sight when blocks of ice appeared from a deep well of water. Several blocks approximately three feet long x two feet wide and about nine inches thick, were hauled from the water by means of a steel cradle, during each production cycle. They were then man handled to a nearby cold store, where they were held until they were required for delivery to the various customers.

The ice factory was operated by Jim Nicklin, who resided in a nearby property. He was a very nice man and a good friend of my father, Robert Pownall, particularly so in their younger days.

Ice making finished in the 1950s and the plant was subsequently sold to an overseas company. The mill itself was partially damaged by fire and then it was demolished.

From Penn Bridge, Bosley Brook flows through Madcroft Wood and then across agricultural land until it enters the River Dane, approximately one mile from Penn Bridge.

Up until the early 1970s, Bosley Brook flowed into the mill pool at Dane Mills, Higher Works, where it contributed to the total water supply required to power another Gilbert Gilkes & Gordon Ltd turbine.

When the decision was taken in the early 1970s to decommission the water turbine at Dane Mills, the mill pool was filled in and Bosley Brook was ducted underground to flow directly into the River Dane.

Penn Bridge, constructed from stone blocks, has a single arch span of 3.66 metres, and it has a load bearing capacity of 40t C&U (Construction & Use Regulations 1986)

As can be seen in the photograph, the bridge was built in 1856 and it possibly replaced an earlier bridge, although it's more than likely that the earliest crossing of Bosley Brook at this location would have been via a ford.

This type of stone bridge was very common in those days and their durability is such that many will still be around for generations to come. Stone is a very strong material in compression and arch bridges are designed to achieve constant compressive stresses, by transforming vertical loads to near horizontal forces, which are supported by robust abutments, also constructed from stone. The arch would have been built around a timber support frame, which would be removed, once all the voussoir blocks and the keystones were securely assembled, and the arch was self-supporting.

Penn Bridge has outer ledges above the arch and beneath the side parapets. As young lads, we spent many happy hours climbing along these ledges, sometimes falling off, but that's how it was in those days!

I occasionally return to this bridge, which had such great importance in my early life.

2
Macclesfield Canal Bridges

There are three bridges along the Macclesfield Canal as it passes through Bosley Village that are very special to me. They are all situated within a 500 yard length of the canal stretching towards Congleton, from midway between number 11 and number 12 of the 12 Bosley Locks.

As a young lad growing up in the village of Bosley, I spent a lot of time in this locality, and these three bridges bring back fond memories of a bygone era.

The first bridge I'm recalling is the railway bridge situated above number twelve lock, which supported the Churnet Valley Railway on the track connecting Bosley and North Rode Stations.

This railway line opened in 1846; therefore the bridge would have been constructed some time before this date.

It is a fabricated steel beam bridge, with the steel sections held together by many round head rivets. There are structural side parapets, plus a central parapet situated between the two sets of rails.

The fabricated steel beam construction is supported either side the canal by substructures, built from blocks of local stone.

The Churnet Valley Railway became a victim of the Lord Beaching closure programme and the line was closed in 1964. Although the steel railway lines were removed, the bridge remains in place as of 2013.

It was on this stretch of the Macclesfield Canal, beneath the railway bridge, and in the basin below lock number eleven, where we did the majority of our fishing. We mainly caught roach using maggots as bait, or perch that we tempted with a nice juicy red earth worm.

The bridge provided shelter when it was raining, and the sound of a steam train passing above, when we were underneath, was something I shall never forget.

I recall a time possibly in the 1960s, when the canal was drained and clearly visible on the mud banks below number eleven lock, was a fine specimen fresh water mollusc. I have never seen anything like it before or since, and I believe it was a Swan Mussel, in the region of four to six inches in length.

In the summer time, Mother Nature provided a special treat, as on the grassy bank adjacent to the bridge substructure on the northern bank, there was always a fine crop of wild strawberries. They were delicious, very sweat when fully ripe, and about the size of a large garden pea. I should like to return to this location at some stage in the future, just to see whether those wild strawberries survive to this day.

I also recall the lock keepers cottage, now demolished, that stood adjacent to lock number eleven. It was a white washed building, and the lockkeepers name was Tom Hartshorne.

Another lasting memory from this location was the abundance of glow worms on the stretch of railway track from the Canal Bridge to Bosley Station. Typically, on a barmy autumn evening, we would be heading for home along the track side, and it was like fairy land, with lots of glow worms shining in the dark.

The second of my three Macclesfield Canal bridges, is the Bosley Aqueduct, which carries the Macclesfield Canal over the River Dane. It is an elegant structure, located 300 yards from lock number twelve, and in 1984, it became a grade two listed building by English Heritage, who gave it an identity reference 58138.

I was always fascinated by this bridge, and of all the bridges described in this book, some of which I have passed over, and others I have passed beneath, this one is unique, as it is the only one that I have swam over.

As young lads in Bosley Village, we would spend a lot of time in the height of summer, swimming in the murky waters of the Macclesfield Canal. Our main location for this activity was by bridge 57 located 150 yards from the aqueduct, in the direction of Congleton.

Very often, we would swim from bridge number 57, the 450 yards to number twelve lock, therefore, crossing the aqueduct along the way.

It is a very ornate structure, engineered by William Crossley Jnr, who was the engineer for the Macclesfield Canal between 1826 & 1833. It is approximately 45 feet high, and it has a span of 35 feet crossing the River Dane. The structure has very pleasing lines with straight sided imposts and pilasters, and outward curving abutments, topped by wrought iron railings that have arrowhead spikes on top.

As well as curving outwards from the straight sided imposts, the abutments also curve downwards, away from the bridge. The arch and imposts have a stone parapet either side of the towpath, and when you look over the top, the River Dane seems a very long way down.

I remember peering over the top of the downstream parapet, one hot summer's day, and I was shocked to see a couple, who were semi-clothed, and sunbathing, on top of a side abutment. They lay flat out, and didn't show any signs of the dangers below if they had taken a fall.

 The third of these three bridges situated along the Macclesfield Canal as it winds its way through the village of Bosley, is bridge number 57, known as Old Driving Lane Bridge.

Presumably, it was constructed to allow cattle to cross the canal at this location.

This is the bridge where the local children swam during the hot summer days. Sometimes there would be just the odd child swimming, but on occasions, I remember there being quite a number of local folks including parents, and often, some would have picnics on the grassy canal bank alongside the bridge.

I remember one such occasion when a teenage local lad appeared on the scene wearing his newly acquired army uniform. He had recently joined the forces, and he was visiting home whilst on leave.

He sat watching the local juveniles, including myself, diving into the canal and generally splashing around. He must have thought to himself how he would like to join in the fun. He made his way to the top of the bridge and appeared a few minutes later, donning nothing more than his army issue under pants. They were snow white and a type of boxer short, coming down to his knees.

He didn't hesitate and dived in to join in the fun. All was well until he decided to leave the water, and as he hauled himself onto the concrete pathway at the side of the bridge, he was extremely embarrassed as the water had made his under pants almost translucent, and the girls as well as a few mums, got a good view of his well-proportioned manhood. When the crowd began falling about laughing, he placed both hands over his crotch and quickly disappeared up onto the bridge to get dressed and regain his decency.

This bridge was a focal location for play, during my childhood days, and its memory stays with me indefinitely. It is where I was taught how to swim, and there is a very amusing story associated with the bridge, but you will need to read my memoirs entitled 'Funny How Things Work Out', to fully appreciate that one!!

The Macclesfield Canal opened in 1831, therefore the aqueduct and bridge number 57 were constructed sometime before that date. The stone required for building these, and other bridges, plus the Bosley Locks, came from a nearby quarry at the end of Bosley Cloud.

Bosley Cloud is a large hill, 1,125 feet high, which overlooks Bosley Village. When I was a lad, there was a tradition that each Good Friday, local folk from nearby villages, and the town of Congleton, would climb to the top of the Cloud, from where there are spectacular views of the surrounding area and across the Cheshire Plain.

I haven't visited these bridges in over fifty years, but their memory is as vivid as ever, and it has given me great pleasure recalling their association with my childhood life.

N.B. The front cover colour photograph of Bosley Aqueduct is by kind permission of author – David Kitching.

3

Foryd Bridge - Rhyl

This bridge named the 'Foryd Bridge' and known locally in Rhyl as the 'Blue Bridge', was opened in 1932. It spans the River Clwyd at the entrance to Rhyl Harbour in North Wales.

The bridge is of steel construction, comprising two bowstring spans, with a central pier. It was designed by R G Whitley and fabricated by the Dorman Long Company, from Middlesbrough, in England.

The wreck in the foreground of the photograph, is the remains of a wooden, three masted, square rigged ship that was named 'The City of Ottawa'. She was constructed in Quebec in 1860, and abandoned in Rhyl in 1906, following considerable storm damage. She was a merchant vessel, built in Quebec City, at the Jean Élie Gingras

Shipyard. She was an all timber ship, weighing 880 tonnes, and she is alleged to have made in excess of thirty world voyages, plus many shorter trips. Her remaining timbers have survived all these years, partially submerged beneath the estuary silt of the River Clwyd.

The reason I have included this bridge is because it brings back very happy childhood memories of family holidays spent in the seaside resort of Rhyl. It also marks the location, where I did a lot of crab fishing, alongside the bridge. I used winkles for bait, as they were in abundance at the water's edge, generally attached to a stone by their mollusc type foot.

The poor winkle wash crushed between two stones and its soft body was attached to the end of my crab line. It was then a matter of casting the line into the harbour, and very soon, there would be a crab clinging to the bait. I would pull it out of the water for safe keeping in my little bucket, until the crabbing session was over. As I recall, these were green coloured crabs and not the edible pink variety.

When I had finished fishing for that day, all the crabs were returned to the harbour, I guess to be caught another day!!

I remember the journey to Rhyl from our family home in Cheshire. We first caught a public transport bus from Bosley Village to Macclesfield. It was then another bus to Crewe, followed by one to Chester, and finally, a bus from Chester to Rhyl. I suppose it took the best part of a full day to get to our holiday destination, but it was always worth it, once we had arrived.

We really enjoyed those holidays, staying in a boarding house, not far from the sea front. There were no en-suite facilities, as we would take for granted nowadays, and the food was from a fixed menu, so you could either take it or leave it. I can remember coming down in the morning and seeing the dining room tables set for breakfast. There were bowls of corn flakes awaiting milk and sugar, and this was followed, some days by a fried breakfast, and on others, it would be a boiled or poached egg.

Life was very simple in those days, and as we didn't know any different, Rhyl was one of the seaside places; we looked forward to visiting, for our one week annual holiday.

4

Conwy Suspension Bridge

Completed in 1826, the Conwy Suspension Bridge was designed and constructed by Thomas Telford.

Spanning the River Conwy, it was built close to the famous Conwy Castle that was constructed much earlier by Edward 1, between 1283 and 1289. It is very similar in design to the Menai Suspension Bridge, some 19 miles away, which is another Thomas Telford Bridge, completed at the same time as the Conwy Suspension Bridge.

The two and a half metre wide deck is suspended from two sets of four chains, which are stacked in vertical alignment, and supported by stone constructed towers, then anchored at each end, into the ground level bed rock.

The bridge once carried the A55 road across the River Conwy, with a span of 99.5 meters.

Such was the traffic congestion, that in 1958, another road bridge was constructed alongside the suspension bridge, providing an additional carriageway for the A55 over the River Conwy, and at this time, the suspension bridge was closed to traffic.

Although the deck of the suspension bridge was replaced in 1896, the iron chains remain the original ones fitted, when the bridge was first constructed.

Between 1986 and 1991, the A55 was re-routed once again, this time by means of a tunnel beneath the Conwy Estuary.

I can recall as a teenager, passing over the suspension bridge and the toll fare was 6d (six pennies) about the equivalent of two and a half pence in today's money.

I have included the iconic Conwy Suspension Bridge because it reminds me of amazingly good holidays during the 1950/60s, spent at the Morfa Caravan Park just beyond Conwy, heading towards Caernarfon.

In those days, most mill workers had one week holiday per annum and where I was serving my engineering apprenticeship, at Wood Treatment Ltd, in Bosley, Cheshire, the dedicated week for our annual leave was the last week in July. With the unreliability of our British weather, I can recall having worked hard for a full year, it would rain persistently during that week, but even so, those holidays were something special.

We generally stayed in a rented caravan on the Morfa Caravan Park, located on the outskirts of Conwy. How well I remember those caravans of that era, in particular, the smell from the gas mantle when it was time to turn on the lights.

Other memories include climbing 'Conwy Mountain' ('Mynydd Dref' in Welsh), from a narrow pathway, opposite the caravan site entrance. It was a hard climb to the top, which is 801 feet above sea level, but the views when you reached the summit, made all the physical effort worthwhile.

Reminiscing about smells, reminds me of the Champion Bakery, located by the side of the caravan site entrance. The wonderful smell of freshly baked bread, together with a bracing sea breeze, never failed to improve your appetite.

Another lasting memory was regular visits to the Ship Inn at Penmaenbach, which was about half a mile from the site, heading towards Penmaemawr. The landlord was an excellent mine host, who served a fine pint of Worthington 'E' bitter, which was always in top condition. I don't recall the landlord's name, but he was a most pleasant man, who had a bristle moustache, and he always remembered me from my previous visits. When the weather was inclement, I have spent a good portion of my holiday in the Ship Inn, getting wet on the inside!!

Sadly the Ship Inn was demolished in 1986 as part of the A55 road improvement scheme.

A holiday in Conwy was never complete without a trip to the top of the 'Great Orme' at nearby Llandudno. I remember during the late 1950s, those occasions, when I visited Randy's bar, which was situated on the Great Orme. The licensee from 1952 to 1961 was the legendary ex-middle weight world boxing champion, Randolph Turpin.

I met him on several occasions during visits to Randy's Bar.

He had an incredible boxing career, with a total of seventy five fights, sixty six wins, of which, forty five were by a knock out finish.

Compared to holidays in this day and age, those spent in Conwy in the 1950s and 1960s seem very basic, but despite this, clear fond memories of those times will remain with me always.

I intend re-visiting Conwy at some stage in the future, to take a stroll across the suspension bridge, which is now owned by the National Trust. It will be something special to look forward to.

5

Duke Street Bridge - Birkenhead

 Duke Street Bridge in Birkenhead, reminds me of my brief service in the Merchant Navy, as its location is adjacent to Vittoria Dock, where Blue Funnel and Sister Company, Glen Line ships, operated from.

It was out of Vittoria Dock that I sailed on board the S.S. 'Talthybius' on her voyage number 43, bound for the Far East.

This type of bridge is known as a bascule bridge and this particular design has a rolling action, which is activated by twin beams connected to a pivot point. As these beams are traversed horizontally by electric motors, the bridge rolls back, lifting the road deck to an almost vertical elevation.

I have written about my service with the Blue Funnel Line, in my memoirs entitled 'Funny How Things Work Out', but I wrote a separate magazine article, which is more specifically about the ship S.S. 'Talthybius', and I'm including it here as in my memory it has a very close association with the Duke Street Bridge in Birkenhead.

S.S. Talthybius 1944 to 1971

I served on the S.S. 'Talthybius' in 1967, when she was operated by the Ocean Steam Ship Co, owners of the famous Blue Funnel Line.

In those days Blue Funnel had a fleet of 82 vessels and ran schedule cargo services from the UK to Australia, and the Far East. They also ran similar services out of New York.

Until the end of 1966, they carried up to 20 passengers per ship; these were generally very wealthy people that would stay with the ship for the entire voyage, which generally meant, three and a half months away from the UK.

S.S. 'Talthybius' was built as a 'Victory' ship, by the United States Maritime Commission, and at the time of her launch in 1944, she was named S.S. Salina.

Victory ships were designed and built to replace merchant cargo vessels that had been sunk during WW2. They were some of the first ships to be manufactured with all welded hulls. They were constructed as modular units and assembled in a matter of six weeks, start to finish. Everything about them was very basic as their life expectancy was quite short. In the main, they were used to convoy supplies to Europe and unfortunately, many never completed the Atlantic crossing, falling victim to enemy torpedoes.

At the end of the war, Blue Funnel purchased six Victory ships from the US Maritime Commission for what was believed to be £1m. Originally, 'Talthybius' was purchased by the Dutch Blue Funnel Company and renamed S.S. Polydorus. In 1960, she was transferred to the UK Blue Funnel Line, at which time she was again renamed, this time to 'Talthybius'.

All Blue Funnel ships where named after characters from Greek Mythology. 'Talthybius' would never have carried passengers, as her accommodation was very small. A typical officer's cabin had a small bunk, a single wardrobe, a small settee, a table, and a single chair. There was a small wash basin but no toilet or shower facility.

Due to the all welded construction, many of these Victory ships suffered severe damage in heavy seas, and in fact some vessels even sank due to fractured hulls.

The Blue Funnel Line never lost a ship in peacetime, and received an excellent reference in Winston Churchill's memoirs.

I joined the Blue Funnel Line as an Assistant Engineering Officer, and following initial training and coasting two main-line vessels, the 'Hector' and the 'Pyrrhus', I was offered either to sail supernumerary to New York on the Queen Mary, and join a Blue Funnel ship named 'Menestheus' destined for the Far East, or to sign on to 'Talthybius', which they were bringing back into service, following several years laid up in the Carrick Rhodes.

The Carrick Rhodes is in Cornwall and comprises a deep natural harbour created by the last ice age. This has long been a place where ships out of service could be laid up for long periods of time.

It was the time of the six-day war between Israel and Egypt and when President Nasser closed the Suez Canal, and Blue Funnel had two ships, the 'Agopenor' and the 'Menelaus', trapped in the Bitter Lakes on the Suez Canal. I was offered the opportunity to serve on one of these ships, whilst they were out of service. There would be increased rates of pay, in recognition of the boredom aspect, as well as the danger of being in a war zone.

I decided to opt for 'Talthybius', as she was bound for the Far East and the excitement of those faraway places was very appealing.

I first met up with 'Talthybius' in Glasgow, and when I arrived at the King George 5th dock, she was a rusty hulk that looked ready for the scrap yard.

She and a sister ship had been brought back into service to replace the two main line ships stranded in the Suez Canal.

Whilst Blue Funnel operated regular services that in the main ran like clockwork, they had tramp steamers that tided up after main line ships, as well as sailing there and back with a full cargo. This was to be the roll of 'Talthybius', and when I was offered the position of Assistant Engineering Officer I was told that we would be away up to five months, and amongst her ports of call would be Shanghai in the PRC (Peoples Republic of China), which at that time was caught up in the Great Proletarian Cultural Revolution, headed by Chairman Mao Zedong.

The thoughts of going to China at this time appealed to me greatly, as it was a closed society and Blue Funnel ships usually called at the British Colony of Hong Kong. This was to be a rare opportunity and I saw it as a great adventure.

When I told some of my colleagues what I had volunteered for, they fell about laughing. I had never seen a Victory ship, and was used to the comforts available to officers on mainline ships, like the 'Hector' and 'Pyrrhus' on which I had completed my initial training. I recall that on board the 'Hector' my accommodation comprised a well fitted out day room with a beautiful roll top desk. There were no port holes, rather, large windows with wonderful views of the open sea. My cabin on 'Talthybius' would have measured no more than 3m x 3m and there was one port hole, which was positioned such that it was useless to view through.

I coasted 'Talthybius' from Glasgow to Swansea in South Wales, where we took on board steel products from nearby British Steel at Port Talbot. We then returned to our homeport of Birkenhead where the remainder of loading took place. It was a work of art in those days prior to containerisation, and specialist teams of stevedores loaded cargo according to where it was destined, and at what stage in the voyage it would be discharged. The ships hold comprised of deep bottom tanks that could either be filled with liquid or dry cargo. Above these tanks were several decks that were individually filled with cargo and then capped off before another deck was completed above. We took on board many products including machinery, motorcars, to things like toothpaste and corn flakes.

When all the holds were full, they then took on board deck cargo mainly comprising barrels of oil. These were strapped down with steel cables for safety and security in the event of heavy weather.

Before we embarked on voyage 43 to the Far East, I was allowed to visit home for one-week leave. Upon my return to the ship, we were all set to go and to my distress I discovered that I had left my uniform black tie at home. I just found time on the Saturday morning to nip to the uniform shop and purchase another one.

Back on board, I was off watch whilst we put to sea, and along with other colleagues, I stood out on deck observing as tugs arrived to guide us out into the River Mersey.

The ship was moving steadily away from the quay, when I spotted a man running down the dock carrying a small parcel and shouting "package for Pownall". As he approached the ship, we were several yards from the dockside, but he threw it as best he could, and it landed not far from where I was standing. It was my original tie that my Mother had posted. It was amazing that it arrived as it was addressed to the ship in Birkenhead.

That episode over, we moved out into the river, right opposite the Liver Buildings, and gradually 'Talthybius' picked up speed, and we were on our way.

With the Suez Canal closed, we were heading down the Atlantic Ocean all the way to Durban, South Africa.

Ports of call in chronological order were as follows: -

Durban – South Africa

Singapore

Jesselton – Borneo

Labuan – Borneo
Manila – Philippines
Cebu – Philippines
Shanghai – China
Moji – Japan
Pusan – South Korea
Singapore
Penang
Port Swettenham – Malaya
Colombo – Ceylon
Trincomalee – Ceylon
Durban – South Africa
Las Palmas – Canary Islands
Liverpool – King George 5th Dock

In those days Blue Funnel only employed white ethnic officers and all other crew were either Chinese or Malaysian. A typical crew was as follows: -

Captain	*Chief Engineer*
First mate	*Second Engineer*
Second mate	*Electrical Officer*
Third mate	*Third Engineer*
Fourth mate	*Fourth Engineer*
Cadets if there were any on board.	*Fifth Engineer*
Radio Officer	*Sixth Engineer*
Chief Steward	*Seventh Engineer*

NB - The fifth sixth and seventh engineers were all ranked as Assistant Engineering Officers. You were graded according to your academic qualifications, engineering experience, plus examinations by the 'Board of Trade'. This determined the amount of seagoing time required before you were able to take the merchant marine engineering examinations.

We had three quartermasters whose job it was to steer the ship. No such thing as automatic steering in those days.
We had a boatswain who was also Malaysian.

The Chinese crew comprised engine room staff, stewards and cooks.

The total number of ship's crew was approximately 60 personnel.
In those days, if the total crew was less than 100 personnel, there was no legal requirement to carry a ship's doctor and in our case, the Chief Steward was in charge of medical matters having obtained a first aid qualification, and he had a very good book for reference purposes.
There was a small hospital on board, which had an operating table, sterilised surgical instruments, and step-by-step pictures to assist in minor operations in the event of an emergency. There was no mortuary on the ship, and we were advised in advanced, that in the event of a death on board, it would be a case of burial at sea.

The role of an Assistant Engineering Officer was mainly a watch keeping activity. This involved monitoring the main and auxiliary engines, maintaining the ships log, and carrying out minor repairs as became necessary. There were regular tasks such as checking the steering mechanism at the end of each watch, and conducting chemical analysis of the boiler water, and dosage as might be necessary, to maintain the correct quality of boiler feed water.

Standby duties involved partaking in the control over the main engine during manoeuvres in and out of port, and the recording of each change of engine speed, plus its direction of rotation, into the ships log. This was an exacting task, which had to be accurate, with the time logged to the nearest second.

Standby duty was a two-man operation, usually involving a senior, plus an assistant engineering officer. One would respond to a request from the bridge for a change to engine speed or direction by manually positioning the engine room telegraph and then entering the change in the engine room manoeuvre log. Answering the telegraph required training, and involved more than might be realised. It wasn't just a matter of aligning the indicating arrow to the new call from the bridge. There are strict rules requiring a swing of the arrow beyond the new position and then back to align with the opposed arrow, operated by the deck officer on the bridge. In addition, there could be emergency calls that required a double swing, and if things became really dangerous regarding the ships speed and movement, there was a red flashing light activated from the bridge that really focused the engine room officers on standby duties.

The other engineer on standby duty opened and closed the steam valves controlling the turbines speed and direction. This was quite strenuous work requiring considerable physical effort.

Watch keeping occurred around the clock, whether or not the ship was at sea or in port. When at sea, the watches were four hours on followed by eight hours off. Each watch was covered by a senior and assistant engineer, but in reality, it was the assistant who spent all his time on watch, actually in the engine room. Senior engineers had other duties that they carried out remotely from the engine room.

With the Blue Funnel Line, each voyage was split into three, one designated outward bound, one designated homeward bound, and the *third was known as the coast. I was teamed with the second engineer outward bound on the four to eight watches. I was with the fourth engineer on the eight to twelve, whilst we were at sea doing the Far Eastern Coast and together with the third engineer on the twelve to four during our voyage home. The watches were hard on the body, as you were in fact going to work twice in every twenty-four hours, and sleep patterns were such that you had two sessions of sleep during a twenty-four hour period.*

Whilst in port, you were on port watches that were different from seagoing watches, and were designed so that each officer had a similar chance of sometime ashore. The Blue Funnel line operated four port watches e.g.

12-00 noon to 17-00 pm	*5 hours on duty*
17-00 pm to 02-00 am	*9 hours on duty*
02-00 am to 08-00 am	*6 hours on duty*
08-00 am to 12-00 noon	*4 hours on duty*

How it worked was, you did one watch and then skipped two, but it meant that your two colleagues were either on watch or sleeping when you were off duty. Time ashore generally meant going without sleep, because each day and every day, whether the ship was at sea or in port, you had to do your eight hours watch duty. Standby duties were additional to watch keeping, and if there was a breakdown, you would be called upon for as long as it took.

Time off with sickness was not an option, I remember having a tooth extracted whilst in Singapore, and it was a very unpleasant experience, leaving me feeling very sore with a gum infection. No excuses, I had to keep my watches even though I was totally exhausted.

Times were equally tough when the ship was in heavy weather. Without stabilisers, the ship could roll up to thirty degrees and pitch like a roller coaster, when heading into huge waves. We faced waves up to sixty feet high off the Cape of Good Hope, which was quite scary. Sleep deprivation took its toll, and at times we were seriously exhausted. Fortunately, bad weather didn't occur that often, and for me, I was lucky that I didn't suffer from seasickness. A lot of it was common sense and those that were regularly sick, used to eat unwisely. In really bad weather the galley was closed and they provided us with a French bread stick and a piece of cheese to munch on.

I lost about 28 pounds with my weight stabilising at about ten stones. My weight loss was not due to a lack of food, it was down to the excessive heat in the engine room and the constant running up and down steep ladders, whilst on watch.

The temperature on the manoeuvring platform was always around 123°F varying only slightly with the external ambient air temperature. There was no such thing as air conditioning on a Victory Ship; instead, air was drawn down from the deck by large fans that distributed it around the ship, including the engine room. Once I had lost my excess weight, I felt very fit except in bad weather when everyone, whether you were seasick or not, felt very tired and generally quite woozy.

Noise was a problem within the engine room mainly coming from the ships engine, which was a Westinghouse triple expansion steam turbine, generating 6,000 horse power, with the high speed shaft rotating at 15,000 rpm (revolutions per minute). When steaming full ahead, it was almost impossible to hold a conversation without shouting into each other's ears. We had no ear protection whatsoever, so I guess many crew members would suffer from deafness later on in their lives.

Health and safety was very limited on board, and as well as no ear protection, there were no hard hats to protect your head from falling objects, or breathing masks to filter out any airborne asbestos from the extensive insulation and lagging, which covered all the steam pipes and valves.

I've already referred to the main engine, which was fed with superheated steam from twin boilers built by Babcock and Wilcox. These provided steam at an operating pressure of 465 psi (pounds per square inch).

Electrical power was produced by turbo generators, of which the turbines were manufactured by Joshua Hendy Iron Works, of San Francisco. The coupled generators had been designed and built by Allis Chalmers of Milwaukee, and they produced 300 kw (kilowatts) of three wire DC (Direct Current) electricity.

The propulsion shaft, which connected the main engine gearbox to the ships propeller, was 16 inches in diameter, and rotated at 100 rpm. This speed and power gave the ship a top speed of 15 knots. Because 'Talthybius' was a relatively old lady and heavily corroded around the deck plates, we ran the prop shaft at 90 rpm, which gave us a normal cruising speed of 11 knots. As well as for safety reasons, it was also more economical and efficient to run at this slower speed. The ships propeller was a four bladed bronze type, weighing 29,765 lbs (13.3 tons) with an outside diameter of 18 feet – 3 inches.

A total of 534 Victory were built in various USA shipyards. 'Talthybius' was built by the Permanente Metals Corp, at their No 1 Yard, Richmond, California. Her hull number was 536 and she was originally named S.S. Salina and launched in 1944.

She had a gross tonnage of 7,713 tons and a displacement weight of 15,200 tons.

Looking back, I am pleased that I had the opportunity of spending what was a short time in the merchant navy and in particular serving with the Blue Funnel Line, who were renowned for being amongst the best shipping companies at that time. Discipline was very strict on board, which was good; however there were certain restrictions that I didn't agree with.

e.g. junior officers, of whom I was one, were not permitted to socialise with senior officers and junior officers plus senior officers, were not allowed to socialise with other members of the ship's crew. I found this nonsensical, and it meant that you spent a lot of time on your own, which did not suit my personality type. Some guys were very content with their own company, but I needed companionship. I did have a drinking partner who was the Electrical Officer, and this was within the ship's rules. He and I would drink together at every opportunity and our regular tipple was beer plus gin & tonics.

On the return part of the voyage, I spent a lot of time off watch teaching one of the Chinese crew how to speak English. The lessons took place in my cabin, and I would give him a couple of beers because he amused me greatly with his pronunciation, particularly with words beginning with 'r' & l'. Not long before we arrived home, I was instructed to stop this socialising with a member of the crew, and despite my objection, I had to comply with the instruction.

One morning, shortly before we arrived home, I was in the 4th Mates cabin, when the steward came round with morning coffee. "I don't believe it" I said, "chocolate biscuits, it's the first time I've seen chocolate biscuits after several months on this ship". "What do you mean?" said the fourth mate; "we have chocolate biscuits every single day". I was furious, as on the engineers deck, we had plain biscuits such as, 'morning coffee' and 'nice' varieties. I immediately went to the Chief Engineers cabin and complained bitterly. He advised me to forget the matter, as I was unlikely to change anything, and as I was leaving the company at the end of the voyage, it would be better all-round, to let sleeping dogs lie.

During the voyage, I had noticed something else, which I considered to be discriminatory and unfair. Each Sunday evening for dinner, we had *prime fillet steak with a fried egg on top. It was obvious that the captain had the largest steak and thereafter, they became slightly smaller as they progressed down the ranks, until at my end of the table, they were noticeably smaller in size. Whilst this was grossly unfair, it didn't make any sense, because it was the lower ranks that were doing the physically demanding duties, whereas the Captain and Chief Engineer mainly had clerical roles to perform. Our electrical officer used to remark that the head cook must spend ages trimming a little off each steak so that they appeared smaller than those given to the immediate senior ranking officer. What a nonsense, and totally at odds with what Blue Funnel had been announcing that as of about 1965, Deck Officers and Engineering Officers, would have equal status, and all signage on the entire fleet had been changed showing only 'Officers', whereas, prior to this, the signs used to read, 'Officers and Engineers'.*

Looking back, I suppose I can understand why these situations arose. After all, Blue Funnel had a very strict discipline on board, and there was social segregation between senior and junior ranks as well as with other members of the ship's crew.

Whilst the Chief Engineer has four stripes as well as the Captain, it is obvious that the Captain is in overall command of the vessel, and what he says, goes.

I recall on one occasion, whilst we were in a Far East port, we were carrying out essential maintenance to one of our steam turbine generators. Having spent many hours stripping the generator down, we received a call from the Captain requesting that we abandon the work, and get the damn thing back together ASAP. All involved in the maintenance task thought the Old Man had lost the plot, and it wasn't until dinner that evening, when he explained that he had been offered a cargo worth £1m in another port that we realised the wisdom of his decision. We could not put to sea without that generator in service, and the quickest action was to abort the maintenance, and put it back as it was, *and then find another opportunity for a maintenance window, later on in the trip.*

Upon our arrival back in the UK, a personnel officer within the company head offices at India Buildings offered me a stint on the Blue Funnel ship 'Centaur'. This was a relatively new vessel that sailed between Singapore and Sydney Australia. I was very tempted, but decided to stick with my decision to move on, as I believed that I didn't have the right aptitude or temperament for a career in the Merchant Navy. I felt very lonely and with working in effect, twice each day whilst at sea, a week seemed like an eternity. It is good to look back, and recall some of the great times, and whilst a career at sea was not for me, I wouldn't have missed the experience for anything.

Although I have complained about some elitism in favour of the deck officers, I must admit that all officers were extremely well looked after. The food was 5 star quality and we went short of nothing. The pay was good, and I found the whole experience character building, particularly so, when visiting those faraway places.

There is an interesting video on 'You Tube', which shows a 9-minute clip of the workings of an engine room of a Victory Ship. It is entitled 'SS American Victory Engine Room'

Sometime after I left the Merchant Navy, 'Talthybius' was transferred to a Sister Company, the 'Elder Dempster Line' and operated on their West Africa service, before being laid up at Bromborough Dock, in Birkenhead. In December 1971, she was broken up by 'Nan Feng Co. of Taipei, Taiwan.

I feel privileged to have spent a short period of my life aboard this splendid vessel.

Now returning my attention back to the Duke Street Bridge, Birkenhead, I am also reminded of a nearby pub named the 'Pilot', where I downed more than a few pints of beer during my training period!!

Assistant Engineering Officer Pownall pictured with Mother Lucy Amelia, whilst on leave in May 1967.

S.S. Talthybius 1946 - 1971

6
Iron Bridge – Shropshire

This unique bridge located at 'Ironbridge Gorge' on the River Severn, in the County of Shropshire, England, was the first arch bridge in the world to be constructed from cast iron.

All of the 800 plus individual castings, the largest of which weighs five tons, were cast at a foundry in nearby Coalbrookdale. Many of the individual castings are assembled to each other by means of Mortise & Tenon, and Dovetail joints, similar to those used in the joinery trade.

Coalbrookdale is claimed to be the birth place of the industrial revolution when Abraham Darby began smelting iron with coke.

The bridge was designed by Thomas Farnolls Pritchard, and it was built by another Abraham Darby, the grandson of the earlier Abraham Darby, who perfected the cast iron smelting process.

The bridge, crossing the River Severn, has a total length of 200 feet, and the cast iron truss arch, has a span of 100 feet. At its highest point, it stands 60 feet above the water below.

Construction of the bridge started in 1779, and it was officially opened on 1st January 1781.

I first became aware of this incredible bridge when I began visiting the area, through my employment as a technical sales representative.

One of my main customers in the region was Ironbridge Power Station, which is not far from the location of the famous Iron Bridge.

It was during the early 1970s that I made weekly visits to both the 'A' & 'B' stations, and it was one of my favourite calls. I made some good friends with the team of mechanical engineers, and it provided a great opportunity for me to increase my knowledge of the Power Generating Industry.

There is a story in my memoirs regarding Ironbridge Power Station, which I believe is well worth repeating here.

The early seventies was a tough period for Pat and me, following the birth of our first child Tracey in 1970.

She was a lovely baby, but not the best when it came to sleeping all night. I was working extremely hard to establish myself with my latest employer, and with many disturbed nights, life was not easy. I remember my area manager saying to me "why do you always appear so knackered?"

I responded by saying, "I'm tired, because I'm working very hard and not getting a lot of sleep."

There was another technical sales representative working alongside me and he decided to move on with another employer. I was asked to spend some time with this guy, whilst he was working his notice period, and each lunch-time after he had eaten his sandwiches, he would loosen his collar and tie, and nod off for about half an hour.

He recommended this to me, as he said it re-charged his batteries, and afterwards, he felt refreshed, and ready to resume his work in the afternoon.

This didn't seem right to me, but several weeks later, I was back on my patch working alone, and it was my weekly visit to Ironbridge Power Station.

As usual, I parked my car in a lay by not far from the station, and after I had consumed my packed lunch, I thought I would try what the other representative had recommended, and I put my head back and closed my eyes.

I had intended taking just forty winks as I was due to visit the station at two o'clock. I must have been particularly tired at that time, and when I woke up and looked at my watch, I nearly died as it was turned half past five in the evening.

I remember thinking I shall get the sack for this, as I guessed when I hadn't arrived at the station, someone would have contacted the office enquiring about my wellbeing. I travelled home worrying that my new boss would sack me if he found out what had happened.

Needless to say, I didn't sleep much at all that night, and as soon as I entered the office the following morning, I asked to see the area manager, privately in his office.

I told him the truth, hoping that he would treat me leniently. He listened intently as I told him the tale, and when I'd finished, he gave me a broad smile and asked me to go about my business.

He obviously respected my contribution to the sales operation, and I felt much better knowing that I had confessed my misdemeanour.

I remember attending the interview for this my first job within a sales department and the area manager asked how I would handle a situation if for some reason the company was unable to supply a crucial component to a customer and as a result, their production levels were being affected.

I didn't give the question a great deal of thought, and I told him I would give them the truth, and equally important, I would explain what we were doing to rectify the situation. He told me that I had given him the answer he was looking for, because if I was to be successful with my job application, it was company policy to always tell the truth.

Obviously, I did get the job, and throughout my 40 years' service with the same employer, that philosophy regarding integrity and honesty, stood me in good stead, in developing and maintaining my business.

7

Tower Bridge London

Photo by David ILIFF. License: CC –BY-SA 3.0

Tower Bridge spanning the River Thames in London, England, is truly, a spectacle to behold.

Technically, Tower Bridge is a combined suspension and bascule bridge, designed by Horace Jones and completed in 1894.

The central span comprises two hydraulically operated bascules, each weighing 1,200 tons. Power to raise the bascules is provided by six hydraulic accumulators, which were originally energised by two 300 horse power, twin tandem, Compound Steam Engines. Boilers provided steam at 80 psi to drive the engines.

In 1974, the original operating mechanism was replaced by a new electro-hydraulic power system.

The two 82 metre suspension spans located either side the opening bascule spans, complete the bridge structure.

At the top of the central bascule spans, there are two pedestrian walkways, which are 44 metres above water level at high tide.

I first visited Tower Bridge in the early 1980s, and after driving over the bridge, I took the opportunity to tour HMS Belfast, which is moored upstream from the bridge, in the Pool of London.

 This was the first and only time I have been on board a naval war ship. My first impression was how compact everything seemed, compared with the Blue Funnel merchant ships, on which I had spent time as a ships engineer. This is a very different vessel, purposely kitted out for high speed manoeuvrability, as well as fighting an enemy with an armoury of powerful weapons.

The crews sleeping quarters are particularly cramped and the engine rooms bear little comparison to that of a merchant cargo ship. It was a very interesting experience, and greatly enhanced by the piped sound effects and commentary, relevant to the part of the vessel you are entering.

HMS Belfast was a Royal Navy Light Cruiser, constructed by Harland & Wolf, Belfast, and launched in 1938.

She was commissioned into the Royal Navy in August 1939, and following a long service period, about which, much has been written, she was finally decommissioned in 1963, and in 1971, she became a museum ship, part of the Imperial War Museum.

A tour of HMS Belfast provides a brilliant insight into what it was like to serve on such an amazing war ship.

8

River Nile Bridges, Cairo

In the mid-1980s, we took a family holiday in Cyprus, staying in an apartment at Paphos. In advance of the holiday, I had planned a trip to Egypt, and towards the end of our first week, we booked an excursion, which involved an overnight sail from Limassol to Port Said, on board the MS Princesa Marissa, operated by Louis Cruise Lines Services.

We arrived in Port Said early the following morning, where there was a coach waiting, to take us the 123 miles to Cairo.

The route took us close by the Suez Canal and I must admit it did look strange seeing ships passing through the dessert. We saw lots of fabulous sand dunes, some of which were more than 30 feet high.

As we arrived in Cairo, we crossed the River Nile over the '6th October Bridge' and I took this photograph from our coach window. I was able to capture an adjacent bridge, half a mile away, and this is the 'Qasr al-Nil Bridge'.

Our first stop in Cairo was a visit to the 'Egypt Museum of Antiquities' located in Tahrir Square. The first thing that struck me upon our arrival in Egypt was how it was a country of contrast, with a wide divide between rich and poor. I recall as our coach pulled up outside the museum, I spotted a guy riding on a donkey and alongside were two extremely wealthy looking guys travelling in a very smart Rolls Royce car.

The exhibits on show within the museum were almost unbelievable and the only down side to the visit was the amount of time allocated for our stay. We only had two hours, therefore we focused upon the King Tutankhamen displays, which are breath taking. I could have spent two days in the museum, but before we knew where we were, it was time to move on.

Back on the coach, we travelled the few miles to Giza, where we were scheduled to visit the pyramids.

I had always had a fascination about the mystery of the pyramids, having read about the speculation as to the secrets they may hide, regarding who actually built them and how. But when you step off the coach, and there before your very eyes, are these unbelievably large structures, the reality of their size truly registers in your mind.

The outside temperature was in excess of 40°C so we were advised to keep our exposer to this extreme heat to a minimum.

There was an opportunity to enter the 'Great Pyramid' by a narrow shaft leading to an internal chamber at the bottom of a steep slope. Pat and I decided to give it a go, and I led the way. There was a great deal of hustle and bustle, with throngs of tourists all having the same idea. There was chaos, partially fuelled by everyone wishing to get out of the intense heat, plus local Bedouins, attempting to herd people along, a little like sheep.

After a short wait, we managed to enter the narrow shaft, and shuffle our stooped bodies down the steep incline. After no more than a few yards inside the passage way, I began to feel very uneasy and somewhat claustrophobic. I glanced round, and Pat was signalling that she was turning back. We both made an on the spot decision, and turned around and fought our way against the flow of incoming visitors.

We had both felt very uncomfortable in those clamped surrounds and our instincts told us we should retreat very quickly.

We moved on to view the nearby Sphinx, which was undergoing some restoration work.

Again, when you actually see something like this, it blows the mind trying to comprehend such amazing creations by mankind, all those centuries ago.

The sheer dimensions of the 'Great Pyramid' are staggering, and for over 3,000 years, at 455 feet high, this was the largest structure on Earth, and when initially constructed the height was 481 feet.

There are many theories about the Pyramids as to whom or what constructed them. There are those who believe, they were built by some form of alien beings as men on Earth all those thousands of years in past, would not have had either the equipment or technology, to undertake such an incredible task.

There are lots of facts about the Pyramids, which are difficult to comprehend. For instance, within the Great Pyramid at Giza, there are hollow channel ways built into the body of the structure that point to a specific constellation in the sky. To achieve this, whoever of whatever built them, must have had building skills beyond our comprehension, plus knowledge of astromany that beggars belief.

We headed back to Port Said where we boarded our cruise ship for our overnight sail back to Limassol in Cyprus. This had been a spectacular holiday so far, but it was now about to take a drastic turn for the worst. I fell ill and ended up in hospital, but I'll leave you to read my memoirs for the full story about that!!

 The River Nile is divided in Cairo by Gezira Island, and the 'Qasr al-Nil Bridge' spans the west side of the river from Gezira Island to Downtown Cairo. The bridge designed by Dorman Long & Co Ltd, was constructed between 1931 & 1933 and it was officially opened on June 6th 1933. The steel structure comprises 7 spans crossing the Nile.

6th October Bridge – Photograph by Author – flyvancity from New York USA

Since our visit to Cairo in the mid-1980s, when we crossed over the '6th October Bridge', it is now part of a much extended elevated highway stretching some 12.7 miles and the complete bridge, now crosses The River Nile at two separate locations.

The name of this bridge commemorates the Yom Kippur War in 1973, between a coalition of Arab States headed by Egypt, against the state Israel, which started on the 6th October 1973 and ended on the 25th of that same month.

I often think of these two bridges whenever I see the news from Cairo. It is a great pity that the country has faced such political turmoil in recent times, and I hope that this great nation with such an incredible history, will soon find a solution to the current unrest.

9

Florida Bridges – USA

Pat and I have enjoyed several holidays in Florida USA, when our children were young, as we wished to visit the Disney World, and other attractions in the Orlando area.

In 1992, Pat and I were planning a holiday, just for the two of us, and we decided to do a fly drive in Florida, with nothing booked except our return flights, plus a hire car.

We spent our first night in the USA, in a hotel close to the Orlando Airport, and then set off to explore the 'Orange State' of Florida.

There are two bridges that we crossed over, which have stayed in my memory, one being the 'Seven Mile Bridge' on [1] US route 1 in the Florida Keys, and the other, is the impressive looking 'Sunshine Skyway Bridge', close to St Petersburg, on the West Coast.

Our travels took us firstly to Cocoa Beach, from where we joined the coastal roads south to Palm Beach, Fort Lauderdale, Miami, Key Largo, and Key West.

Everything went well except for our one night stay at Palm Beach. As we were approaching the town, the weather became most inclement as a tropical storm was approaching. The rain was so heavy that it became difficult driving the car, and we had to focus upon finding some accommodation for the night. We spotted a sign for a travel lodge and pulled over to check if they had vacant rooms. As we entered the reception area, it was apparent that this was a fairly basic hotel, but as the weather was now becoming a little scary, we decided to check-in.

We had not eaten since breakfast, so our first priority was to get some food. There was nothing available at the lodge, so we looked around the immediate vicinity, but there were no eating houses within easy reach. It wasn't safe to take the car, so we came to the conclusion that we would need to take shelter in our very basic hotel room until the storm subsided.

We kept looking outside, but the storm continued to rage until well after dark. We didn't consider it safe to venture out as there were individuals peering around corners of nearby buildings, which was somewhat intimidating.

Our only means of sustenance was a bottle of Scotch whisky that I had brought with me in my suitcase. As there was still a gale blowing outside and the rain was lashing against the windows, we kept having another Scotch and water, and after a couple of hours of drinking on an empty stomach, we were rather tipsy.

We didn't feel secure in this place as there were individuals wandering around outside, which seemed a little strange in such bad weather conditions.

Just to be on the safe side, I decided to barricade the door with a chair and then with all the Scotch now consumed, we turned in for the night.

As I lay in bed, I thought it might be prudent to hide my wallet in case we were burgled during the night. I found a suitable place and returned to our bed, and the next thing we knew it was morning.

It was a great relief to see that the storm had now abated, and although there was still a strong gale blowing, the rain had stopped and once again there was a blue sky.

We decided to check out and head south as soon as we could. Pat was tidying up and packing our suitcases, and I was studying the map and planning our journey for the day. As always, before leaving a hotel, I was completing my routine check, making sure that our passports and important paperwork were all present before making our departure. All was fine until I checked on my wallet, and panic set in because I was unable to find it. I told Pat we had been robbed and asked her to report the matter to the reception, and request they call the police.

She had just left the room, when I remembered that I had hidden the damn wallet, and due the amount of booze on an empty stomach, I had completely forgotten all about that. I was able to shout to Pat before she reached reception, so we were spared any unnecessary embarrassment, but Pat was not pleased, and she gave me a lecture about the dangers of drink!!

Our fly drive continued and when we arrived at Key West, we decided to stay for a period of five days. It was a wonderful place, but now it was time to head north and our next destination was a visit to the Everglades. It was a long drive, but by around lunchtime we arrived at a nature reserve visitors centre, where I hoped to take a ride on an airboat. I made my way to the reception area, where upon, I enquired about an airboat ride. The attendant gave me a somewhat repugnant look and said there were no airboats on their reserve as they were a menace to wild animals. He told me the only way I could take a boat ride on the Everglades in that area was to travel 60 miles south where they hired out boats, but they were certainly not airboats.

We gave the matter some thought and although it was going to add another 120 miles to our mileage for the day, we headed south and after about an hour, we found the location where you could hire out little motor boats.

When I enquired about hiring a boat, I was informed that they only hired these boats to individuals who had experience of handling motor powered vessels. I told a little white lie, and soon we were in the boat and heading out onto the large expanse of open water. Pat was very uneasy about the entire thing, and as she is a non-swimmer, she was afraid of the boat capsizing as well as being eaten alive by a huge alligator!!

We didn't have to sail far before we spotted several alligators, some of which were fearsome looking beasts. I assured Pat they were more afraid of us than we were of them, but I do admit that there were a couple of times when I worried about our safety. There were swarms of midges in the air, and we were badly bitten, so after about an hour exploring the surrounding Everglades, we returned our boat and resumed our journey north.

Our next stop was Naples, followed by Sarasota and St Petersburg, from where we returned to Orlando. In total we travelled 1,300 miles in our hire car, and we thoroughly enjoyed all the places we visited.

On the last day back in Orlando, we decided to visit Disney World on a one day pass, on the proviso that Pat would join me on a couple of roller coaster rides. Pat was 46 years of age at the time, and she had never had a roller coaster ride in her life, always preferring to watch, whilst I, and our two children had all the fun.

We pretended to dress up like a couple of teenagers and off we went to Disney. The first ride I managed to drag Pat onto, was the 'Runaway Train' and I was pleasantly surprised, when she got off saying it wasn't as bad as she had feared.

Now with much more confidence, Pat volunteered for the 'Black Hole', not realising what she was letting herself in for. I sat in the front of Pat in a carriage, and as we were taking the terrific ride, I was laughing all the time, as she was swearing out loud in a most uncommon fashion. I recall her expression, (You b*****d Pownall)!!

This had been an exciting day, bringing to an end, a most amazing holiday/vacation, which neither of us would ever forget.

This is an aerial photograph of the seven mile bridge that Pat and I crossed on our journey along ⒧ US route 1 to visit Key West.

This is a box girder structure, built from reinforced concrete. It comprises 440 spans and connects 'Little Duck Key' with 'Knights Key' in Munroe County, Florida.

The actual length of the bridge is 6.79 miles, with a raised central arch section, to allow the passage of marine traffic.

The bridge opened on May 24th 1982 and alongside, there are the remains of an earlier bridge, which opened in 1912.

This is the 'Sunshine Skyway Bridge' which spans Tampa Bay, Florida. It is a cable stayed design bridge with a main span of 1,200 feet. The total length of the bridge is 4.1 miles and it carries highway ⒭ US route 275. There are 42 stayed cables per pylon; each clad in 9 inch diameter steel tubes.

10

Forth Rail Bridge – Scotland

When I first set eyes on this bridge in the late 1990s, I considered it an awe inspiring structure, both from its spectacular size on the landscape, as well as the complexity of its design. We have all seen photographs of this world famous bridge, but it's not until you stand in close proximity of the vast cantilever structure that its true magnificent splendour can be fully appreciated.

Completed in 1890 to span the 'Firth of Forth' at Queensferry in Scotland, this fine example of Victorian engineering stands proud in memory of Sir John Fowler and Sir Benjamin Baker, the two men who are attributed with its complex design. To think that such an enormous fabricated structure could have been planned, let alone constructed without the aid of computers and modern day technology, simply blows your mind.

The total span of this bridge is 8,296 feet, which includes the two longest sections of 1,710 feet each.

It took circa 58,000 tonnes of steel to build the complete bridge, and until the Quebec Bridge was constructed in Canada, the Forth Rail Bridge had the longest cantilever span anywhere in the world.

Sadly 90 men lost their lives during the build programme, which is not surprising when you consider the sheer scale of the structure, and with 5,000 construction workers employed, during its assembly.

The bridge carries two rail tracks, some 46 metres above the water level at high tide.

Pat and I were on holiday, staying at the 'Caravan Club Site' located at Queensferry Road, Edinburgh. We had towed our touring caravan from Worksop, and this was our base from where we intended visiting local points of interest.

Apart from Edinburgh itself, our main priority was to visit the Royal Yacht Britannia, which is now a museum ship, berthed in the nearby Port of Leith.

As we approached 'Britannia' at her mooring, her visual impact was outstanding. Her sleek lines and her elegantly shaped funnel, and three tall masts, are instantly recognisable.

We boarded the Royal Yacht and found the whole experience enthralling. You have the opportunity of viewing many of the state rooms including, the State Dining Room, the Royal Bedrooms, the Queens Sitting Room, the State Drawing Room, the Ships Hospital, and the engine room is visible through a glass viewing panel.

There are many of the original artefacts including the grand piano, which Princess Margaret enjoyed playing, as did, Princess Diana and occasional guest, Sir Noel Coward.

The open decks are constructed of solid teak, and the entire ship has a quality of build that is second to none.

Britannia was commissioned by Queen Elizabeth II father, King George the VI, on 4th February 1952, and ironically, he sadly died just two days later.

She was built by John Brown Company of Clydebank, Scotland, at a cost on £2,098,000, and she was launched by the Queen on 16th April 1953.

This famous ship saw 44 years' service as the Royal Yacht, having been commissioned on 11th January 1954, and finally, decommissioned on 11th December 1997.

She sailed over one million nautical miles, with 696 overseas visits and 272 home visits.

Britannia has a gross tonnage of 5,769 tonnes, she is 412 feet in length, has a beam of 55 feet, and a draught of 15 feet.

She was powered by steam turbines, which generated 12,000 horse power giving her a speed of 21.5 knots, plus a range of circa 2,400 nautical miles.

Britannia in my mind is one of the finest ships ever to sail the high seas, and it is easy to appreciate the sadness shown by the Queen when the Royal Yacht was taken out of service. Long may she continue to serve as a museum ship, and bring much pleasure to the many foreign and home visitors, who flock to experience the viewing of this amazing vessel.

The Royal Yacht Britannia photographed in Portsmouth
By Steve Daniels

11

The Humber Bridge – Hull

The Humber Suspension Bridge is the largest suspension bridge in the United Kingdom, and high up in the list of the longest bridges of its type in the entire world.

The bridge reminds me of two separate periods in my life, the first being the time when I was managing regional offices in both Leeds and Hull.

Each Monday morning, I would drive from Leeds to Hull taking the M62 Motorway followed by the A63 to the centre of Hull. In the evening, I would travel home to Worksop, and I always gave the great suspension bridge a second glance as I passed by. Somehow, it looks almost unreal, and I marvelled at how it was constructed on such a grand scale of bridge building technology.

The other reminder relates to the later years of my full time employment, when I made the decision to use Humberside Airport as the starting point for my long haul travel. It is such a pleasant airport with modern facilities, and without the hassle of much larger UK regional airports. When travelling to the USA and China and South Korea, I would take the KLM City Hopper from Humberside Airport to Schiphol International Airport in Amsterdam, from where I took a direct flight to my long haul destination. Although Schiphol is a very large airport, I find it extremely user friendly, and it is an easy airport in which to find your way around.

When taking off from Humberside Airport, I always made sure that I got a good view of the Humber Bridge, whenever the take-off direction took us towards the bridge in the Humber Estuary.

At that time, KLM were operating three types of Fokker Aircraft on their regional connecting flights, namely the Fokker 50, Fokker 75 & Fokker 100.

The Fokker 50 is a turbo propeller aircraft and for some reason, I was always pleased on those occasions when this aircraft arrived at Humberside for our short hop to Schiphol. I suppose I realised that this old design of aeroplane was approaching the end of its operational life, and I considered it a privilege to have the opportunity to experience the thrill of this type of aviation travel. The cabin was noisy, but I found it exhilarating and it made a perfect start and finish to a business trip, whenever the Fokker 50 was in service.

Following my retirement I took Pat on a holiday to China and in advance of the trip, I told her that I hoped our flight to Schiphol would be on board a Fokker 50. I can picture us now sitting in the executive lounge at Humberside Airport and my thrill when I spotted a KLM Fokker 50 coming into land.

That was to be my last ever opportunity to fly with a KLM City Hopper Fokker 50, as in March 2010, the last remaining two aircraft were retired from service.

The Humber Bridge, which opened to traffic in June 1981 effectively made the hitherto ferry service between Hull and New Holland redundant.

Ferries began operating from Hull to New Holland in 1826 and some of the paddle steamers in service over the years included – P.S. Magna Carta, P.S. Wingfield Castle, P.S. Tattershall Castle, & P.S. Lincoln Castle.

Some details about the Humber Suspension Bridge:-

- Spans the Humber Estuary connecting Hessle, East Riding of Yorkshire, with North Lincolnshire.
- Carries the A15 highway.
- The main span is 1,410 meters in length.
- The north side span is 280 metres & the south side span is 530 metres in length.
- The deck width including pathways/sidewalks is 28.5 metres.
- Clearance over high water is 30 metres.
- Diameter of the main suspension cables is 0.68 metres.
- The load in each cable is 19,400 tonnes.
- The two suspension cables comprise 14,948 x 5mm diameter wires, plus an additional 800 similar wires to each cable on the northern side span.
- The 150 feet vertical towers are 34 mm wider apart at the top to take into account the earth's curvature.
- Weight of steel in the bridge is 27,500 tonnes.
- Weight of concrete used in the construction is 480,000 tonnes.

12

Royal Border Bridge

This photograph shows a train crossing the Royal Border Bridge, which spans the River Tweed at Berwick upon Tweed. This Victorian bridge is an incredible structure, built mainly from stone blocks, plus some bricks in the construction of the arches.

There are a total of 28 semi-circular arches, each having a span of 61.5 feet. 13 arches span the River Tweed, with the remaining 15 arches, built across dry land south of the river.

I have visited this famous bridge on numerous occasions, whilst on holiday in the area, and the very first time I stood beneath one on its arches, I peered upwards and gasped with amazement. The sheer height of the stone supports becomes very apparent when you are up close. The bridge was opened on 29th August 1850 by Their Royal Highnesses

Queen Victoria and Price Albert, following several years of construction.

The total length of the bridge is 2,160 feet and it is 126 feet high at its highest point, and it is now an English Heritage, grade 1 listed building, ID ref 1393563.

Before building the huge stone support columns could commence, the construction engineers had to pile the gravel laden subterranean ground with elm wood piles, to a depth approaching 40 feet. This major piling operation was carried out by means of 'Nasmyth's Patented Steam Powered Pile Hammer. I find it astonishing that such pioneering engineering practices were in use all those years ago.

Pat and I have enjoyed a walk, upstream from the bridge on two separate occasions. There is a trail alongside the river's edge leading several miles, and the scenery is something special. At one time there was a thriving salmon fishing activity, along this section of the Tweed. In fact on our very first visit to Berwick, we saw salmon fishing taking place, by a net stretched between two small rowing boats.

On each of our visits we stayed at the Seaview Caravan Club Site in Spittal, Nr Berwick, which offers fabulous sea views. Berwick has a small port and I used to enjoy seeing the occasional small ship enter the estuary from the vantage point of our caravan window.

The Royal Border Bridge carries the main East Coast Railway Line, which operates high speed trains, and the northerly approach to the bridge passes close by the caravan site, where the noise of the trains gives a real sense of high velocity, dynamic motion. These trains then have to brake hard before crossing the bridge as obvious speed limits are in force, as well as the Berwick-Upon-Tweed Railway Station.

Berwick is a very interesting town, with historic remains to explore, including the Castle ruins and the Ramparts, complete with some of the original cannons situated in strategic locations.

Just a few miles south of Berwick-Upon-Tweed is 'Lindisfarne' also known as 'Holy Island'. We have visited this island on two occasions and found it a fascinating place, which has historic records of early Christianity, dating back to the sixth century.

You access the island by a causeway at low tide, and you have to gauge the time of your return to coincide with the timetable of local tides. The causeway, which is several miles long, becomes completely covered by the North Sea twice each day, by several feet of water. On both our visits, we managed to stay approximately three hours, so we needed the two trips to see all the points of interest.

English Heritage owns the site of the ruins of 'Lindisfarne Priory', which is a must for your visit, as is, the 'Lindisfarne Castle', now owned by the National Trust. Many of the rooms within the castle are set out as they were when it was last occupied by a private owner.

The island offers magnificent walks, the only constraint for us was time, ensuring that we crossed over to the mainland, before the causeway became flooded once again.

On one of our visits to Berwick-Upon-Tweed, we witnessed a partial eclipse of the sun, which was a somewhat weird experience. We had just parked the car in a local shopping area, when the eclipse began, and the first thing we noticed was birds in flight, rapidly taking to their roost. The daylight started to fade and the summer air temperature took an immediate dive. I personally was pleased when it was over as I felt something strange and unnatural taking place and quite frankly, it gave me the creeps!! Fortunately, it was soon over and I was pleased to see the seagulls and pigeons, once more taking flight.

Berwick-Upon-Tweed is a great place to visit, and a walk beneath an arch of the 'Royal Border Bridge' makes you appreciate the immense skills of our Victorian engineers.

Finally, out of interest, the railway engine passing over the 'Royal Border Bridge', in the photograph, is the steam locomotive Nº 60163

'Tornado', which was built in Darlington by the 'A1 Steam Locomotive Trust', and completed in 2008. It is a replica of the famous (LNER) Peppercom Class A1 locomotive, of which 49 originals were built, but unfortunately, they were all scrapped when British Railways discontinued using steam locomotives.

N° 60163 Tornado operates regular rail services and the details can be found by means of the A1 Locomotive Trust website.

13

Cross Keys Bridge - Sutton Bridge

Located in Lincolnshire, England, 'Cross Keys Bridge' is a swing bridge, which allows the passage of boats and small ships along the River Nene, at the Village of Sutton Bridge.

Nowadays, the bridge carries two lanes of the A17 highway, but when it was constructed in 1897, it had just one carriageway for road vehicles, plus a single railway track, which was used by the Midland & Great Northern Railway Company. When the rail branch line closed in 1959, the bridge was converted to the present day layout.

It was constructed from steel girders, made by the 'Staffordshire Steel Company' of Bilston, England. Originally, it was operated by water hydraulics, powered by Armstrong Whitworth three cylinder oscillating engines, and nowadays, the rotating mechanism is driven by a more modern oil powered hydraulic system.

The 176 feet span, swings 90° to allow the passage of river traffic, providing access from the North Sea, to the port town of Wisbech.

The reason for including 'Cross Keys Bridge' is because it reminds me of enjoyable caravan holidays at Sandringham, where The Caravan Club have a splendid site, situated on land leased from The Queen's Estate. Each time we towed our touring caravan from our home town of

Worksop to Sandringham, we passed over 'Cross Keys Bridge', which represented a landmark as we approached our holiday destination. Each time I drove over the bridge I was always impressed by how pleasing it appears on the eye. It stands regal on the landscape, and represents a fine piece of nineteenth century engineering and architectural construction.

We always looked forward to visiting Sandringham, where we enjoyed long walks in the estate grounds, and visits to the nearby seaside town of Hunstanton.

No holiday was complete without a visit to the church on the estate. This is where Her Majesty the Queen, Prince Philip and other members of the Royal Family worship, when they are in residence at Sandringham House. We have all seen them on television when they attend this lovely little church on Christmas morning.

Whilst Pat and I are not regular church goers, we get great pleasure from visiting churches, and this has been one of our all-time favourites.

It is only a small building, but it has character with its very ornate solid silver alter and pulpit.

The surrounding grave yard provides a resting place for many of the deceased estate workers, some of whom spent their entire working life serving the reigning monarch in some capacity or other.

This is a postcard showing 'Cross Keys Bridge' as it was originally built, with a single lane highway, plus a rail track.

14

Makaranga Garden Lodge Hotel - Japanese Garden Bridge
South Africa

With a span of just a few feet, this is the smallest bridge featured in my book. However, it's none the less important for that, as it invokes very fond memories of my two business trips to South Africa.

This little stone bridge can be found within the Japanese garden, which forms part of a thirty acre nature reserve at the Makaranga Garden Lodge Hotel.

I shall never forget the place, and I rate it amongst the best hotels where I have stayed, during all my global business travels.

The hotel is situated in Kloof, which is approximately 16 miles from Durban, and following a hard day, travelling and conducting business, this is an amazing retreat, where you can stroll around the extensive grounds, taking in the wonderful atmosphere, made special by all the interesting flora and fauna.

I clearly recall seeing lots of Ibis and the dawn chorus from many species of wild birds is something you never forget.

I remember standing on top of the little bridge and pausing to listen carefully to the trickling stream passing beneath, plus all the other natural noises, making up an orchestra of pleasing sounds, all conducive to cleansing the soul.

My first visit to South Africa began with a flight to Cape Town, and from there, I travelled by car along the coastal road in a northerly direction to Saldanha, where my business colleague and I stayed at a very nice hotel, with fabulous views of Saldanha Bay.

We broke our journey several times to view locals selling all manner of hand crafted goods, also at other interesting spots including, Whale watching locations. At one such stop we encountered a troop of Baboons who were begging for food. There were signs warning against feeding these wild animals as they are potentially dangerous. We also saw many wild ostriches running at great speed amongst the surrounding countryside.

Prior to my trip, my daughter had been watching a morning TV program, which was broadcast live from South Africa. She had seen those road side stalls selling their wares, and she asked me to purchase a Giraffe, hand carved from local hard wood that she intended to position by the side of her fireplace. At one of our stops I was able to buy a suitable Giraffe, and that gave me great pleasure.

Following our business calls in Saldanha, we returned to Cape Town, where we had some free time for sight-seeing before we were scheduled to fly to Durban.

Cape Town is a fabulous city, overlooked by the iconic Table Mountain. I remember us taking an alfresco lunch at a smart restaurant adjacent to the marina. Our table was located alongside the sea front railings, and as I was tucking in to my chicken and chips, two gulls landed on the railings and they sat their watching me and my colleague feeding our faces. I couldn't quite finish all my chips and just as I had placed my cutlery on the plate, one of the gulls stepped onto our table, and in a flash, the remaining chips had all been devoured. Not content with a few chips, it then picked up the remains of my chicken leg, which was mainly bone, and in front of my very eyes, it swallowed the lot whole. It was an astonishing sight as it was not a very large sea bird, but down went the leg bones after a couple of heavy gulps.

Durban is another splendid city, with lots to see and do, and well worth a visit for anyone intending a vacation in South Africa.

It is renowned for its famous 'Golden Mile' of promenade and sandy beach. With lifeguards and shark nets in place, it is a surfer's paradise, provided by giant rollers, coming ashore from the Indian Ocean.

I was taken to the uShaka Marine World Theme Park in Durban, which contains restaurants' a water park, including seal shows.

The highlight of the visit was the uShaka Marine World Ship Wreck Aquarium, which is an incredible feature. The aquarium itself is housed within the wreck of a 1930s 265 feet long freighter. The rusty hulk looks amazing, and once you step on board there are many fine exhibits for viewing.

We visited other interesting places, whilst in the Durban area, including a crocodile farm, a theme park called 'The Zulu Kingdom' and the '1000 Hills Craft Village'.

The crocodile farm was very interesting, and not only are you able to view crocs at close quarter, but there is a fine collection of indigenous snakes on display. I was amazed to see for the first time, a crocodile actually enter the water. It's easy to see how you can easily be caught out by a cunning crocodile, because as it entered the water from a mud bank, there was hardly a ripple on the surface of the water and no sound whatsoever.

'The Zulu Kingdom' offers splendid live shows of Zulu dancing and war chanting, by performers in native costume. There are numerous exhibits of traditional Zulu huts etc.

To view one of the main performances, the audience are accommodated within a shelter to provide a rest bite from the fierce South Africa sunshine. My host and I took the back seat, which was fine but there was not a great deal of head room. The participant performers appeared in front of us, and when one of the actors banged on his big drum, the noise was so loud that in shock, I shot out of my seat and cracked my head on the roof of the shelter. I felt a fool, but the incident brought much amusement to those sitting close by!!

Our tour of '1000 Hills Craft Village' was another very interesting experience. I was particularly attracted to a little shop named 'Wood Magic' where a guy was carving puzzles from local hard woods. There were many types of carved puzzles on display, which I found intriguing. They are a kind of jigsaw and there are various degrees of complexity. The basic type is a single layer similar to a conventional jigsaw, without the interlocking tabs, but then there are multiple layered types, where the horizontal separations are also shaped, and this greatly increase the puzzle element of assembling all the pieces together.

I couldn't resist making a purchase, and I am now the proud owner of puzzle number 4590. It comprises a single layer puzzle, housed into a carved rhinoceros. It is a splendid piece of craft work and it takes pride of place within the display cabinet in my study.

From Durban we travelled by car to Pietermaritzburg, and from there onwards to Newcastle. Following business meetings at both places it was back to Durban for a flight to Johannesburg, which was my last destination before my return home.

It was a couple of years later when my second trip took place, and on that occasion I flew into Durban via Johannesburg, where I was able to spend several more nights at the fabulous Makaranga Garden Lodge Hotel.

Following customer calls in the Durban area, my business colleague and I took a flight to Johannesburg, from where we to visit several major iron & steel plants.

We then returned to Durban and travelled by car some 105 miles north to Richards Bay. This is a delightful seaside resort with a number of Aluminium Smelting plants located close by.

With all our business calls in Richards Bay completed, it was Friday evening and we travelled a further 52 miles to 'Hluhluwe', where we were to take in a safari tour.

We stayed overnight at 'Sand Forest Lodge' which is a most pleasant recreational retreat.

The grounds comprise a small nature reserve with some indigenous animals that belong to the hotel, and it certainly gets you in the mood for a safari trip in the wild.

Dinner was prepared alfresco style in a small kitchen attached to the grounds, and after a few gin and tonics, roasted chicken, went down a treat.

As we were due to make an early start the following day, we retired soon after 10-00 pm. The chalet was compact but comfortable, and after climbing into my bed, I took great care to tuck in the mosquito net that was suspended from the ceiling.

After enjoying a night cap from the mini bar, I decided to settle off and a couple of hours later, there came a knock at my chalet door. I climbed out of bed and shouted "who is it". "It's me, the hotel owner", was the reply. "What's the matter?" I asked. "If you care to come outdoors, I can show you some special wildlife" he said.

I quickly dressed and stepped out of the chalet, where the owner of the establishment, stood holding a large torch. He beckoned me to follow him to some nearby trees and he shone a beam of light to one of the high branches. He told me there was a large eagle owl up there, and sure enough it stood out, particularly so, with the reflection of light from its large piercing eyes.

The noises in the immediate area were enchanting. He took me to a water hole in the hotel grounds, where there was a host of frogs, croaking their heads off. As they bellowed out those loud shrieking sounds, large balloons of stretched skin bulged out from their cheeks.

He then led me to another location where there were numerous giant black beetles, wandering around in the dark. I wasn't very keen when he picked one up in his hand and offered it to me to handle. It was bigger than a golf ball and an amazing creature, and despite my fear of a bite, I escaped unhurt!!

Afterwards, I returned to my chalet and that's where I did receive a few bites. Although I took great care to tuck in my mosquito net, when I awoke at dawn, I was badly bitten, mainly around my ankles. I guess the mosquitoes had penetrated my bed, whilst I had been out observing the local wildlife.

This morning was a very early start as we were booked onto a safari trip in the 'Hluhluwe' Game Reserve, which meant us leaving our hotel at 05-30 am.

It was just a three hour trip by Land Rover within the game reserve, but it was most worthwhile as well as being a memorable experience. It's obviously the luck of the draw as to the type's game you encounter, and we were fortunate to get close to Elephants, Rhino, Buffalo, Giraffes and much more, but unfortunately, we didn't find any large cats.

I shall never forget when we had stopped for a picnic style breakfast, and an ant crawled onto the table. This was no ordinary ant and without any exaggeration whatsoever, I can tell you it was at least 25 mm in length.

I enjoyed both my trips to South Africa and hope to return on holiday at some stage. I found the people extremely friendly, the climate most pleasant, and in my opinion, the country has a unique culture, all of its own.

I managed to purchase another of those splendid hand carved giraffes, so now my daughter Tracey has a giraffe either side of her marble fireplace!!

We did see the townships around Cape Town and Johannesburg and clearly, there is still a lot of work to be done in the creation of a more equal society, but politics aside, I can only go by what I experienced during my two trips, and I have to say, it is one of the most fascinating countries, I have been fortunate enough to visit.

15

Nanpu Bridge - Shanghai

The 'Nanpu Bridge', located in Shanghai was completed in 1991. It is a cable-stayed design bridge, constructed from concrete and steel and it spans the Huangpu River, connecting the Shanghai districts of Puxi and Pudong. The total length of this huge bridge is 8,346 metres, with a central span of 423 metres.

The cables supporting the deck are connected to two 150 metre high concrete towers. The main deck carries six lanes of traffic and there is a two metre wide sidewalk on either side of the bridge.

 This photograph shows a section of the complex layout of the spiral highway, approaching the bridge from the Puxi side of the river.

The Nanpu Bridge in Shanghai triggers very fond memories about my numerous business trips to China. It also brings back many recollections from the trip that Pat and I made to Shanghai in May 2009. The details of this trip soon after my retirement are recorded in some detail in my book entitled 'Onwards and Upwards'.

Shanghai nowadays, is a very different city to how it was at the time of my first ever, visit to China in 1967. The Pudong district was just wasteland at that time, with none of the sky scraper buildings that now dominate the sky line of this amazing modern city.

I have written a magazine article about my trip to Shanghai in 1967, whilst I was a serving officer in the Merchant Navy, and I have decided to include it here.

A Trip to Shanghai in 1967

We sailed from Birkenhead in June 1967, and because the Suez Canal was closed following the six day war between Israel and Egypt, we had to take a much longer route via South Africa and the 'Cape of Good Hope'. We made numerous stops in the Far East before setting course for Shanghai.

As we entered the estuary of the Yangtze River, we were boarded by a number of 'Red Guards' who were to escort our ship for the duration of our visit. Prior to entering Chinese waters, our Captain had briefed us on how we should conduct ourselves and to remember at all times that we were representing our country; therefore, if we were to encounter any hostilities, we should always conduct ourselves like officers and gentlemen. We were instructed to leave everything inside our cabins unlocked, including our porthole that would normally be tightly secured, whilst we were in any port. All personal possessions had to be left inside a draw and we were assured that nothing would be stolen, whilst we were in China. Our personal radios and cameras were collected by the Chief Steward who locked them all away until our visit was completed. We would not be allowed to communicate with our families or friends, and we were asked to inform our next of kin that we would be incommunicado for at least five weeks.

From the Yangtze we steamed up the Huangpu River, where we were to lay off at a mooring buoy outside the port of Shanghai. We spent a couple of weeks before receiving a signal to go alongside to discharge our cargo of tin plate, which we had shipped from a steel mill in South Wales. When the ship berthed, we could hear the sound of a loud voice coming from speakers attached to telegraph poles on the quay side. In very clear English the voice was making propaganda statements about the British such as "Down with British Imperialism". A sentry box was positioned at the bottom of the ships gangway, where a soldier stood to check the credentials of everyone boarding or leaving the ship. We were advised that shore leave would be permitted, but we would only be allowed to visit either the Seamen's Mission or the Seamen's Shop, located in nearby Shanghai. There was a procedure for leaving the ship, which involved advising the deck officer of the day that you wished to go ashore, and he would then request a car via the Chinese soldier on the quay-side. The car was always a black saloon provided free of charge by the Chinese authorities. I first visited the Seamen's shop where you could buy wonderful things such as camphor wood chests and many items of craft ware. I purchased a couple of fine looking harmonica's as presents for my two young nephews and I would have loved to have taken home a splendid blanket chest for my mother, but I had insufficient room inside my very small officers cabin in which to store one.

My next visit ashore was to the Seamen's Mission, which boasted the longest bar in the world. It certainly was a very long bar, but all we could purchase was Shanghai beer, which was poured from pint sized bottles. It tasted very good, but left me with a terrible headache, when I woke up the following morning.

Having visited the only permitted venues ashore, I decide that once was sufficient and I would now look forward to our next port of call in Japan, where there would be lots of nice girls to chat up!!

We had been in Shanghai for over a week, and I had just come off watch at 08.00 am in the morning, when I was summoned to the Chief Engineers cabin. He informed me that I had been nominated along with three other officers to be guests of the Chinese Government who had offered to entertain us for the day. I was very tired having just come off watch, as it was extremely hot down in the engine room at the height of the Shanghai summer. I had lost a lot of weight and was generally feeling quite weak. All I wanted to do was have a few beers, a good meal, and go to my bed. The Chief would have none of it, he said I should go and get smartly dressed in civilian clothes and prepare for their arrival at 09.00 am.

The four of us stood at the top of the gangway, when our hosts arrived, surprisingly in a coach capable of carrying, I guess 20 to 30 passengers. We boarded the coach and we were invited to sit alongside each other on the rear seat. There were two or three Chinese hosts who shook our hands and presented each of us with a copy of Mao Zedong's famous Red Book. We were also given several Mao lapel badges, which we were asked to pin onto our shirts.

The coach set off and we turned several corners before it pulled up alongside a nearby Dutch vessel. A party of about twelve Dutch Merchant Navy seamen boarded the coach, and I was amazed to see that a number of them had cameras slung over their shoulders. We had been informed by our Captain that photography in Communist China was strictly forbidden that's why all our cameras had been locked away, whilst we were visiting the country.

Our Chinese hosts paid no attention to the cameras, and following the welcoming formalities for the Dutch sailors, we set off for wherever they were to take us. We travelled out of the built up areas and into the surrounding countryside. We passed by a cotton plantation and then visited a number of paddy fields. It was very picturesque and interesting, but really hot on the coach, as of course, there was no air conditioning in those days.

We headed back towards the city, whereupon we were taken to see an industrial exhibition intended to show the world some remarkable technical achievements in China, under the stewardship of Chairman Mao. I had seen this exhibition featured on UK television, when United States President, Richard Nixon had been in attendance, during his state visit to China.

We saw a shiny red tractor that looked remarkably like a Massey Ferguson and a micron beam telescope through which we were invited to view a human hair. Needless to say the hair looked like a tree trunk under such powerful magnification.

We were then shown some steel pressure containers used to store high-pressure gases and a cigarette-manufacturing machine, which was discharging packets of twenty by the dozen.

Finally, we were assembled in a conference room and given a presentation about the technical achievements in China during Chairman Mao's term of office. It was very boastful and Mao's name was repeated in almost every spoken sentence.

Following the presentation, we were given a cigarette, which tasted awful, and a glass of water that was heavily chlorinated and quite offensive to the pallet. We felt we should have to drink the water so as not to offend our hosts, but a colleague muttered in my ear "don't empty your glass otherwise they will fill it up again".

Eventually, with great relief, we were back on the coach and told that we would now be returning to our respective ships as the tour was finished. On our way back to the dock area, we passed a recently constructed stadium that was a spectacular sight, with red flags hoisted all the way round the top of this impressive oval shaped structure. Our Dutch companions were leaning out of the coach windows getting some splendid shots with their flashy cameras. Again, I couldn't believe my eyes in view of the fact that photography was strictly forbidden, particularly so, at the height of the Cultural Revolution.

We passed beyond the stadium, and we were approaching the entrance to the docks, when we heard the sound of claxon horns and very soon, we were overtaken by a number of military vehicles, which forced our coach to pull over and stop at the roadside. Soldiers with rifles were positioned around the coach, and our driver, plus our Chinese hosts, were physically man handled and driven off in another vehicle. A soldier came onto the coach and sat in driver's seat, but said nothing to any of us. You could hear a pin drop on the coach as it was obvious that we had been caught up in some awkward situation, over which we had no control. Cigarettes were being lit one after another as we sat there wondering what would happen next. I was getting more and more anxious as it was beginning to get dark and I was due on watch at 17.00 pm, but there was nothing I could do to return to the ship. We could see 'Talthybius' in the distance and as darkness descended, you could see the funnel lights illuminating the famous black topped blue funnel. One of my colleagues went to the front of the coach and asked the soldier sat in the driver's seat, why were we being detained. The soldier just waved *his arms, suggesting that my colleague should return to his seat. We were now very concerned about how this situation would end. All our cigarettes had gone, and we were in desperate need of the toilet.*

I guess in total we were held for several hours including at least one hour of complete darkness. We then noticed a large saloon car pull up alongside, and four men in long coats got out and walked towards our coach. They came on board and one asked if there were any British Officers present, to which we four on the rear seat shouted "here" .One of the guys approached us and asked if we were in possession of any cameras and of course we said "no". He then apologised for our detention, and said we were free to leave and walk back to our ship.

We were so relieved to get away, and it was wonderful to be back on board 'Talthybius'. We were debriefed by the Chief Engineer and the Captain and I said that there was no way that I would get off the ship again until we arrived in Japan.

Several days later, we put to sea and I can clearly recall seeing the Red Guards leave the ship by means of the pilot boat. It was good to be free once again and now heading for some fun and freedom in a very different culture.

Whilst I have been critical of the Chinese situation in 1967, I have been back to Shanghai numerous times in a business capacity. I have been fortunate to travel to many of China's major cities and I now have a very different view to the one back in 1967.

They are very nice people, hardworking, and exceptionally innovative. Since my retirement, I have returned to Shanghai on vacation with my wife Pat. We had a wonderful time and hope to revisit at some stage.

Approximately one year ago, I received an email from a guy in New Zealand who said he had been searching the Internet and whilst browsing the 'Blue Funnel Association' website, he had seen my blog posting. He was the guy who was sat next to me on that coach all those years ago. He asked whether I remembered him, to which I responded,

"Please read my memoirs 'Funny How Things Work Out' and you are in there"!!

He reminded me of a catch phrase that I started on that voyage, and he quoted it in his email. I have recently completed another book and the title is that same catch phrase 'This is the Life', from all those years ago.

It would be nice if I could meet up with him at some stage, as we now keep in touch.

Having spent many hours trying to trace any fellow crew members on that memorable voyage, all to no avail, I was thrilled beyond belief when he contacted me.

You never know what you'll find in the inbox, and isn't it exciting?

16

Bandra - Worli Sea Link - Mumbai

When I made my one and only visit to India in September 2007, The Bandra-Worli Sea Link was still under construction.

The main section of the bridge is a cable stayed design with concrete viaducts either side, all making up a total length of 5.6 kilometres. The two longest spans, each stretch 250 metres.

The bridge was designed by Seshadri Srinivasan and it spans Mahim Bay, connecting the Bandra district in the western suburbs of Mumbai, with Worli in South Mumbai.

Construction of the bridge began in the year 2000 and ended in March 2010.

My trip to India began with a flight into Mumbai International Airport, where there was supposed to be a car waiting to take me to my hotel. As I entered the arrivals hall, the place was manic with throngs of people, many of whom were shouting out loud, offering taxis to weary travellers.

I waited for a while as I had never been let down before, and I was convinced that if I remained patient, I would eventually see someone waving a sign bearing my name. Alas, it didn't happen, so rather than take just any taxi on offer; my senses told me to seek advice from a policeman. He directed me to a car rental booth in the arrivals hall and they arranged for a taxi to take me and a colleague to our hotel for the night.

We were booked into the 'Sahara Star Hotel' located not too far from the airport. It is a five star hotel, but when we arrived it didn't appear anything special from the external facade. It is a circular building and in the dark it looked a bit grim.

However, once we stepped foot inside the reception area, the place took on a very different image. All the rooms face inward onto a central area, which you could easily mistake for a garden of paradise. There are many tropical plants including palm trees, plus water features, all making a wonderful environment in which to relax. Each of the five star rooms has a balcony overlooking the central garden complex, and I was soon chilling out in a solid teak reclining chair, with a gin and tonic to add to the experience!!

The hotel has a glass roof that takes on the appearance of a starlit sky at night and the effects are simply amazing. I spent a couple of nights in this fabulous hotel before it was time to move on. I had two customer visits to make, one not too far away in the district of Thame and a longer journey by road to the city of Silvassa.

We travelled to Silvassa in a chauffeur driven 4 x 4 vehicle, which was as well, because once we moved away from the Mumbai suburbs, the road conditions deteriorated dramatically, and for the remainder of the 175 kilometre journey, our driver had to be constantly alert to avoid pot holes in the highway, the likes of which, I've never experienced before.

Despite the horrendous road conditions and regular stops to allow cattle to have their privileged right of way, we passed through some most scenic countryside, which was quite hilly in places, and according to out hosts, the kind of terrain where you would likely encounter wild tigers.

We pulled into a motorway restaurant for lunch, and I noticed that our driver sat at a table some distance away from us. I asked our host why this should be and he somewhat dismissed my question by saying that he would prefer to dine alone. I then realised that this was something associated with the cast system in India and I insisted that he should join us at our table. He was a very nice guy and I wanted him to be with us at all stages of the trip. That wasn't to be, but on other occasions, I worked on him and his boss, and by the end of our trip to Silvassa, our driver was eating with us and he didn't seem to have a problem. The cast system is a culture that will take time to fade out completely, but as India continues to develop at an astonishing rate, there will in my opinion, be more equality between the social classes.

We journeyed back to Mumbai the following evening and as darkness fell, we approached the city outskirts. It was scary to see very large trucks, some with lights that looked no more than bicycle lamps and others were displaying no lights at all.

Back in Mumbai, we checked into the 'Sun & Sand' Hotel located alongside Mumbai Beach. This was another five star hotel with prices to match. Gin and tonics were minimal, as at circa £8 per shot, my expense account would not take the strain!!

We were escorted to the Mumbai waterfront during a period of no business appointments, and this proved to be a most interesting experience. I had heard about the 'Gateway to India' beforehand, but until you stand in front of it, you cannot appreciate its true significance on the landscape.

Situated in the Apollo Bunder area of South Mumbai, the 'Gateway of India' is an impressive looking monument, constructed to commemorate the visit by their majesties, King George V & Queen Mary in 1911. It is a basalt arch standing 85 feet high, overlooking the Arabian Sea, not far from the famous Taj Mahal Palace Hotel.

We strolled along the promenade, which was bustling with people selling their wares, including novelty toy items, the likes of which I had not seen before. These ranged from little magnets that when thrown into the air, made a sound like crackling electricity, to enormous balloons, and some creatures made from a jelly type plastic, and when you threw them at the ground, they flattened out before recovering to their original shape.

There was a great atmosphere and everyone seemed happy, although I guess a good many of the locals would be quite poor, possibly living in nothing better than slums.

We made our way to the Taj Mahal Palace Hotel, where our host treated us to afternoon tea. This was a most pleasant experience and I was very pleased that I would not be required to pick up the bill. The hotel is opulent, boasting one of the largest single piece carpets anywhere in the world. Many famous people have stayed at this fine hotel including John and Jackie Kennedy, The Rolling Stones, The Beetles, plus many more, and it's easy to appreciate why.

I really enjoyed my visit to India and hope to return at some stage to share the experience with my wife Pat. One thing I shall never forget was seeing an Indian gentleman in the swimming pool. It was early morning and I observed this man lying in the pool, with only his nose above the surface of the water. His legs and arms appeared to be in a folded position and I assumed he was practicing some kind of yoga relaxation.

On my final day, I took a ride in a tuk tuk, asking the driver to take me to a nearby market. These are those three wheeled vehicles that appear in their thousands, on the streets of Mumbai and many cities throughout the Far East. They are little more than a tiny motorcar body built around a scooter, and like a motor bicycle, the driver steers using handle bars.

In the evening, I took a solitary walk along the Mumbai Beach, which was fascinating and also a kind of spiritual experience. There were lots of people selling superbly crafted jewellery and ornaments, and as the sun began to set, I felt very much at peace with my surroundings. I cannot explain it any better than that, but I guess, it's all to do with the magic of India.

17

Jozef Pilsudski Bridge – Krakow

I made two business trips to Poland during the period when I was working in the metallurgical industries, and it was during my first trip that I visited both Warsaw and Krakow.

I spent a number of nights in a Krakow Hotel, from where I travelled daily to steel plants approximately one hour drive away. Krakow is the most interesting city one can imagine. It is steeped in history and there is just so much to see, particularly for anyone interested in ancient buildings and churches.

There are numerous bridges in Krakow, spanning the Vistula River, but I selected one with a WW2 history.

The Jozef Pilsudski Bridge was constructed in 1933. It is named after Marshall Joseph Pilsudski, who is considered to be the father of Polish independence in 1918.

It is a fabricated steel arch bridge with a 150 metre span, and an overall width of 19 metres.

It was blown up in January 1945 by retreating German troops, but it was rebuilt in 1948.

During my free time, mainly from mid-afternoon onwards I visited as many churches as I could, but the one which stands out in my memory is the Cracow Cathedral, which has one of its outer domes covered in solid gold leaf, and houses the silver coffin of St Stanislaus. Other churches in the near locality include – The Franciscan Church, The Dominican Church, The Church of St Albert, St Mary's Church, The University Church of St Anne, The Church of the Holy Cross, The Church of St Catherine. I didn't manage to visit them all, but it's my intention to return at a later date and enter those that I've missed so far.

Although occupied by Germany during WW2, remarkably, there was no damage to the splendid historic Krakow buildings, many of which house priceless treasures.

The former capitol of Poland, Krakow, or Cracow, is a most beautiful city and it is known as the cradle of Polish statehood and culture. It has several University Schools, Theatres, and an Opera Philharmonic Society.

The main market square is an incredible place, surrounded by impressive buildings and dominated by the Town Hall Tower, which stands dominant at the top of the square. There are numerous restaurants around the square, serving multi-national cuisine, including Polish delicacies such as Golonka, which is stewed pork knuckle or hock, and this proved to be my favourite dish during the trips.

One of my hosts insisted on accompanying all our meals, apart from breakfast, with liberal amounts of Polish vodka. I'm not a fan of vodka, but I must admit that some of those we tried were most pleasant upon the pallet. I did however, decline from upholding Polish tradition of downing a glass full of vodka in one swallow. Firstly, I thought it might burn my gullet and upset my digestion, and secondly, I considered it a gross waste, to gulp something as pleasant as this in one go, therefore, I much preferred to take it in small sips, thereby prolonging the pleasurable experience.

Towards the end of my first visit to Poland I was escorted to the Auschwitz concentration camp, which proved to be a sobering and emotional experience.

We had a guided tour of the camp, which remains unchanged from the time it was liberated on 27th January 1945, by Soviet Army troops. To me, the place had a sense of horror, the likes of which I have never experienced before. There were a lot of Japanese tourists visiting on that day, and I shall always remember the look of disbelief upon their faces. Everyone bore a facial expression of shock and sadness. What took place at Auschwitz was wicked beyond belief.

Our tour began at the railway track, where trains full of unsuspecting Jews arrived, unaware of their forthcoming fate. From the beginning of 1942 until 1945, 1.1 million inmates were put to death, 90% of whom were Jews.

We moved on to view the gas chambers, where the majority of executions took place. Close by, are the crematorium ovens, where the bodies were disposed of.

Our tour also included some of the inmates' quarters, including dormitories, which housed thin badly soiled mattresses, lay on the ground in very close proximity of each other, and this gave a graphic impression of the squalled conditions under which prisoners had to endure. Those that weren't executed upon arrival at the camp had to work hard, and many of these were eventually put to their death.

There are piles of spectacles and shoes, just as they had been left all those years before.

It was an unforgettable experience, which affected my sleep patterns for some period afterwards, but by far the most moving sight of all, was a little girl's dress that she had removed prior to walking to the death wall, where she was shot dead. This was something very disturbing and almost too much to bear.

It's difficult to understand the mentality of those who carried out such atrocities, and if it was possible, I believe every living person nowadays should visit one of these concentration camps, where the realities and evidence, of man's capabilities, regarding inhumanities towards fellow human beings, can be witnessed, if not understood.

18

Charles Bridge - Prague

This most ornate bridge reminds me of a trip I made to the Czech Republic a couple of years before my retirement. I flew into Berlin where I was met by a business college who was to drive me the 313 miles to the town of (Zdar nad Sazavou) in the Czech Republic.

Although I had made numerous business trips to Germany, mainly to Hilchenbach, this was my first time in Berlin, and my colleague kindly offered to show me the sights of this famous city before commencing our long journey by car.

The first point of interest was the location of 'Checkpoint Charlie', which has such historic significance during the period of German separation. Shortly afterwards, we passed a remaining section of the 'Berlin Wall' that is maintained, complete with its original graffiti, as a monument to the past.

It was then off to see the 'Brandenburg Gate', which is a sight to behold. I have to admit that in my mind, prior to this visit, there was an association with WW2, whenever I saw an image of this world famous landmark. We have all seen the vintage newsreel footage of Hitler's procession through the gate and the Swastika Flag draped beneath the triumphal arch, but regardless of this, the impressive architectural monument is no doubt, an awe inspiring structure.

I found it easy to visualise some of the many famous people who have visited the historic monument, including several US Presidents who have made speeches, at its location.

There are many impressive buildings in Berlin, but the one that left an everlasting impression with me, was the 'Reichstag Building', which is the seat of the German Parliament. Its glass dome is an incredible structure, which dominates the skyline as you approach this remarkable edifice.

Time was moving on and we had to commence our long journey into the Czech Republic. We travelled at high speed as is the German custom, but I tried to relax as best I could, and appreciate the splendid countryside. I explained to my colleague that when I was in my adolescent years, we had a German friend of the family, who had been taken prisoner during WW2. He was one of many who were detained in England and he spent some time as an agricultural labourer, working on the land. After the war ended, he decided to stay in Britain, and when I knew him, he worked for a local farmer in the Cheshire village of Bosley.

He was a very nice guy by the name of Anton Johan Franz Riha or (Tony) as we knew him, and we had many interesting discussions. He never spoke about his wartime experiences, but he often referred to his original home, which was located in Sudetenland, now a region in the Czech Republic, known as (Bohemia and Moravia).

Our route was to take us through this region, and it was just as picturesque as our friend had described it, all those years before. Why he had chosen to settle in Britain after the war, I don't know, but following his untimely death following a motoring accident in 1981, his body was repatriated to his native homeland for internment. I felt a little emotional as the beautiful countryside brought back memories of this special guy, who was well liked, and respected, by all who knew him.

Three and a half hours of high speed driving and we arrived at our hotel in the town of 'Zdar nad Sazavou'. It was the hotel 'Penzion Najdek', a most pleasant looking building, with white exterior walls, and a bright red tiled roof. We ate well that evening, and the beer was also very good!!

The following day, I had the privilege of visiting a major engineering manufacturing company, which was extremely interesting, and a place where my colleague enjoyed substantial sales.

After we had completed our business in the area, it was time to head for the ancient city of Prague, from where I was to catch my return flight to England.

My colleague had built time into our programme to show me around the city, before dropping me off at the airport.

Prague is a very popular mini break holiday destination and it easy to see why.

As we drove along the embankment of the River Vltava, there was bridge after bridge. For a person like me who has a fascination with bridges, Prague is a paradise, just for the sight of those amazing structures.

The bridge I selected to feature here is the Charles Bridge, but others included – Legion Bridge, Mans Bridge, Vysehrad Bridge, Jirase Bridge, Libe Bridge, Hlavka Bridge & Nusle Bridge.

We took lunch at a restaurant in an elevated location, from where we had splendid views of the city, including the 'Charles Bridge' and the 'Old Royal Palace'.

The initial construction of 'Charles Bridge' dates back to 1357. Built from sandstone and named after Emperor Charles IV, it comprises 16 magnificent shaped arches, which stretch 516m across the Vltava River. It really is a most splendid sight with its many statues and ornate street lamps.

Prague is definitely on my list of places to re-visit in the future, and next time, I shall spend much more time appreciating the magnificent buildings and spectacular bridges.

19

Incheon Bridge – South Korea

When I last visited South Korea in 2008, the Incheon Bridge was still under construction, but I was able to see the structure at that stage, as my taxi transported me between Incheon International Airport and the capitol city of South Korea, Seoul.

This is an amazing fete of engineering, comprising a cable stayed section, with a main span of 800 metres, and 260 metre and 80 metre spans either side. There are numerous approach spans to the cable stayed section, which are balanced cantilever design spans. The remainder of the bridge is made up of viaduct sections, giving a total bridge length of 12.3 miles. The bridge carries six motorway lanes of traffic, connecting New Sondo City, and the Metropolitan District of Seoul, with Incheon International Airport on Yongjing Island. The build programme commenced in 2005 and completion was achieved by 2009.

My first visit to Seoul in 2008, was in the month of February, and the weather was very cold. I stayed at the splendid Mayfield Hotel, which was extremely comfortable.

My business host took me sightseeing to a nearby theme park, where there were numerous historic Buddhist Temples, all preserved in amazing condition.

With the exception of the Mayfield Hotel, where I only took breakfast, I have to admit that I didn't really get along with the food in South Korea. For lunch and dinner throughout my week long stay, we ate at restaurants, and the menu was much the same. Sometimes I could select some kind of soup for lunch, but in the evening, dinner comprised a barbeque type meal cooked at the table. In South Korea, you usually sit on a cushion at floor level, with your lower legs down in a pit beneath a low level table. I didn't find this particularly uncomfortable, but I would have preferred to have been sat in a chair with a back support.

In the centre of the table, there was a fire bucket and griddle, upon which your meal was prepared. Steak was always on the menu, and the table waitress would cook it in front of you, a small amount at a time. You select the pieces of meat you wish to purchase, and then she keeps returning to the table with the meat, and with a pair of scissors, she snips a piece off, onto the wire cooking tray. Sometimes we had mushrooms as well, and they too, were cooked in the same way, but there was little else, apart from an accompanying salad. I always found the meat as tough as leather, however, by this time, we would have consumed copious amounts of various types of alcohol, which somewhat eased the situation.

After dinner, my business colleague and host insisted upon us visiting a whisky bar. I hadn't realised such places existed, and couldn't believe my eyes when we stepped foot inside. There was a large bar comprising numerous shelves, all filled with many types of whisky, but nothing else. I was shocked when I spotted the prices, as the cheapest bottle of scotch available was $150 US or £100 GBP for something like a 70cl bottle of Bells blended whisky.

Prices went up as high as £500 and more for special brands of single malt.

A single measure or a shot of scotch wasn't an option, therefore, it was a bottle or nothing, but if you didn't manage to finish it off, you could leave the part bottle behind the bar, and return at a later date to finish it off.

Back at the Mayfield Hotel, I was amazed to see Magpies nesting in tall trees in the hotel grounds. This was February, and there was snow on the ground, but the hotel staff informed me that the birds preferred to rear their young at this time of year, as the summers are very hot indeed.

Our main business calls were to be in the city of Pusan, which we reached by an internal flight with Korean Airways.

I had visited Pusan many years before in 1967, whist serving as an engineering officer on the Blue Funnel Ship 'Talthybius'.

Like most of the places I have re-visited many years later, they bear little resemblance to how they were, the first time round.

South Korea is an impressive country, with a vibrant economy, mainly centred upon high technology industries. The people seem very prosperous as indeed they need to be with the cost of living as high as it is.

What a contrast with neighbouring North Korea, which you are able to view from tall buildings in Seoul.

I was very impressed with the numerous iron and steel plants that we visited. The manufacturing equipment is state of the art, and they are producing some of the finest quality steel, anywhere in the world.

Following my retirement, I decided that when we required a new car, it would be a KIA manufactured in South Korea, and now Pat and I are the proud owners of a KIA Venga, which is a pleasure to drive.

93

20

Sydney Harbour Bridge

Although I have written about Sydney Harbour Bridge in the sequel to my memoirs entitled 'Onwards and Upwards', I felt compelled to include this magnificent structure in my book about bridges. I'm avoiding going over the same ground again, and my recollections here are specifically about the bridge itself. The above photograph was taken just a couple of hours after Pat and I landed in Australia. It was shot from the roof terrace of the Holiday Inn, located in the Rocks area of Sydney.

I was very disappointed that we didn't get an aerial view of the bridge when we came in to land, as I would have loved to have seen it from the aircraft.

When I first viewed the bridge, I shall always remember thinking 'Wow' what an amazing sight, and such an incredible structure. Of all the bridges recorded in this book, in my heart of hearts, Sydney has to be the most iconic, and the one I would select if I was forced into declaring my overall favourite. Apart from its sheer size, I found the bridge captivating on the eye, and I spent a lot of time simply gazing at the structure, from as many different angles that were available.

This photograph of Pat was taken from the pedestrian approach to the bridge, just around the corner from the Rocks area.

On our first full day in Sydney, we took a walk over the bridge and this turned out to be a most memorable experience. There are various organised walks on the bridge, but we decided the most strenuous one that involved a climb to the top of the arch, plus other less arduous options, would be too much for us, so we took the easy choice, and strolled across, along the dedicated pedestrian walkway.

The views were simply breath taking and we were very surprised how few sightseers were around. From about half way across the bridge, there are incredible views of the Opera House, with photo opportunities to die for.

We enjoyed the walk across the bridge so much that we repeated it later on in the week.

After a few days sightseeing, we booked an excursion to the Blue Mountains, travelling all the way there by coach, but we selected something different for our return journey to Sydney. We left the coach close by the Olympic Games Centre at a passenger wharf on the Parramatta River, and there we boarded a high speed catamaran for the few remaining miles back to Sydney. This was an exhilarating experience and as we approached Sydney Harbour, the views of the bridge were fantastic.

This shot was taken from the front of the catamaran as we made our final approach. We were able to take photographs from the other side of the bridge when we travelled by ferry for our second week of the holiday, which was located in Manly Beach.

As we passed beneath the bridge, the sheer scale of this very large structure became even more apparent.

The thought came into my head about the number of famous ships that have sailed under this bridge including the Blue Funnel Ship the 'Hector' which I sailed on board in the UK in 1967, when serving in the Merchant Navy.

This is a post card photograph taken of 'Hector', passing beneath the Sydney Harbour Bridge, possibly during the 1950s,

I joined Hector in Liverpool, and sailed to Glasgow, where she discharged her cargo of butter and fresh fruit, which she had transported all the way from Australia.

We had been discharging our cargo in King George IV dock in Glasgow and I needed to go into the city for some shopping items. At that time there was a lot of trouble with anti-social behaviour, and a very serious attack took place on a small child in a pram. The famous singer a film star 'Frankie Vaughn' who did much good work with 'Boys Brigade' was asked to visit the area and try talk a little sense into some of the local offenders.

Our Captain had instructed us to avoid using public transport, so I hailed a local cab into the city centre. When I returned a few hours later, I couldn't believe my eyes when I entered the dock and 'Hector' had gone. I made enquiries, and the harbour master informed me that the ship had moved at very short notice to Elderslie Dry Dock, where she was going to undergo some routine maintenance as well as have her hull re-painted. It cost me a small fortune in taxi fares, as I had to hail yet another cab to re-join the ship on the other side of the River Clyde!!

I took this photograph in dry Elderslie Dry Dock. You can see an engineer stood on the scaffold in the bottom right hand corner of the shot, as maintenance to the propeller and rudder post is being carried out.

This shot shows painting in progress. I was amazed to observe that a team of men painted the entire hull in little more than three hours. They had huge baths of paint, which was applied by hand held rollers, about three feet wide.

Sydney Harbour Bridge was opened in 1932 following almost six years of construction. The bridge was designed and built by Dorman Long

Company who also supplied the majority of the special grade steel from their rolling mills in the North East of England.

The steel sections were fabricated in local workshops in Australia, before they were assembled onto the main bridge structure. It took many fasteners, plus several million rivets to attach all the struts and hangers to the various steel components, which included plate, beams and rods, all assembled like a giant Meccano construction.

Much has already been written about the complex design of this twin through arch bridge, but I shall detail a number of facts and figures as follows:-

Design – Through arch bridge construction.

Spans – Port Jackson, whose main contributory is the Parramatta River.

Total length – 1,149 metres.

Width – 49 metres.

Height – 134 metres.

Clearance below – 49 metres.

The span of the arch – 503 metres.

Weight of the steel arch – 39,000 tons.

Carries – trains, plus eight highway lanes, bicycle and pedestrian lanes.

At each end of the arch there are twin 89 metre tall concrete pylons, which are faced with granite.

Our trip to Australia was one of our finest holidays to date, and my thrill of viewing the famous bridge for the first time, was one of life's most memorable experiences.

21

The Bridge of Sighs - Venice

Located in Venice, Italy, this 36 feet long bridge spans the Rio di Palazzo (Palace River), joining the New Prison to the Doge's Palace.

The bridge was designed by Antoni Contoni, and it was built in 1602, having taken two years to construct.

The name 'Bridge of Sighs' comes from the common belief that prisoners would sigh as they got their final glimpse of beautiful Venice, when they crossed over the bridge, heading for the cells, or the executioner.

Constructed from white limestone, the bridge is very ornate and shines brightly in the Venetian sunshine.

Legend has it that if a couple kiss each other whilst taking a gondola ride beneath the bridge at twilight; they will be blessed with eternal love. It sounds a good story, but it's probably more to do with encouraging couples to take a gondola ride, than based upon any known fact!!

Pat and I visited Venice in 2012 at which time I took the above photograph. It had been our intention to take a gondola ride, but when we saw the cost at £90, we decided to forgo the pleasure. I decided I would buy her a Cornetto ice cream, and sing to her instead!!

We had arrived early morning, whilst taking a P&O Eastern Mediterranean cruise. Having already decided against a very expensive gondola ride, we took a motor launch from the cruise ship terminal, along the Grand Canal to St Mark's Square, which at £15 for the return trip, seemed very good value.

We did our own thing, exploring the narrow streets and taking in all the historic sights. Truly, Venice is a unique city with a culture all of its own. Prices are very high, where you can easily pay £20 for two cups of coffee.

At the end of our stay, it was a splendid experience as our ship sailed along the Grand Canal on its way to the open sea. From the deck of a large cruise ship you get to see all the famous water front sights as well as the many types of vessels navigating this very busy waterway.

Although Venice is a very interesting place, I was a little disappointed as there was a lot of flooding particularly in St Mark's Square, which made getting around somewhat difficult. In places we had to walk across elevated duck boards, which proved a little hazardous.

I was also put off by an unsavoury smell, coming from the water and the awful tat memorabilia for sale at the waterfront. On the contrary, there are many high class shops selling extremely expensive designer goods, plus a Ferrari shop, if you feel inclined to part with >£100k!!

Nevertheless, it was one of the places that Pat and I wanted to visit and I don't wish to spoil it for anyone who has so far not been to this historic city. We enjoyed seeing the sights and I had the opportunity of photographing the world famous Bridge of Sighs.

Things are changing in Venice, and soon, very large cruise ships will no longer be allowed to sail along the Grand Canal to the cruise ship terminal, and this will reduce the amount of boat wake erosion to waterside buildings.

In addition to the restriction of very large ships passing along the Grand Canal, the major project of installing a complex flood defence system will be completed, and this should eliminate the problems that we experienced with local flooding. We hope to re-visit Venice at some stage and no doubt it will appear in a better light!!

22

Öresund Bridge – Scandinavia

The Öresund Bridge connects the west coast of Sweden with Denmark. The overall link comprises a bridge and a tunnel on the Danish side. The bridge stretches 7,845 metres from the Swedish mainland, to a man-made island within the Strait of Öresund, named 'Peberholm', and from there, a tunnel completes the connection with the Danish Island of 'Amager'.

The bridge section is made up of a central cable stayed span over a navigable channel, plus approach sections either side. It was constructed by Hochtief, Skanska, Hojghaard & Schultz, and Monberg & Thorsen, opening on 1st July 2000.

There are two deck levels to the bridge, with the upper one carrying four highway lanes, and the lower deck supports two railway tracks.

The longest span is 490 metres and the maximum clearance below the lower deck is 57 metres.

Pat and I have passed beneath the Öresund Bridge twice, whilst taking a Baltic cruise, and although it is an amazing structure, I hadn't intended including it in this book, as I don't have any related stories. Our visits to the capitals of Sweden and Denmark i.e. Stockholm and Copenhagen, respectively, are covered quite comprehensively in my recent book entitled 'This is the Life', so it's not appropriate to repeat those details here. However, I was prompted to include the bridge and tunnel connection, when I saw a recent BBC television program entitled 'Great Continental Railway Journeys', presented by Michael Portillo. He travelled across the bridge by rail and it seemed such a remarkable experience, that I decided it should now be included in my collection of bridges. Pat and I are avid followers of Michael's railway journeys, where he follows Bradshaw's guides for reference purposes.

It was during the hours of darkness, when Pat and I sailed beneath this bridge, whilst on board the P&O cruise ship 'Azura'.

On the first occasion when we were sailing south, it was about 12-30 am as we were approaching the bridge. We were lying in bed enjoying a night cap, when we spotted an unusual pattern of lights on our cabin television, which was tuned to the ships forward looking camera. We soon realised that it was the 'Öresund Bridge' ahead, and as we got closer it was a spectacular sight, which we shall always remember. As we made our final approach to the bridge, we were able to see the headlights from a heavy stream of traffic travelling across, in both directions. Upon reflection, we should have got ourselves dressed and visited the open decks from where we would have viewed this splendid bridge directly.

This colossus engineering achievement must offer major financial benefit to the countries it connects, as well as the entire region, plus, it provides a fantastic tourist link for the travelling public.

23

The 25 de Abril Bridge - Lisbon

MSC Splendida passing beneath (The 25 de Abril Bridge) June 2011

Pat and I passed beneath this splendid suspension bridge when on board the P&O cruise ship 'Ventura' in 2010. The bridge spans the Tagas River, connecting Lisbon to Almada.

The bridge has two decks, with the upper level carrying six lanes of traffic, and there are two railway tracks on the lower deck.

The total length of the bridge is 2,277.64 metres, with the longest span stretching 1,012.88 metres. Clearance below the bridge at mean high tide is 70 metres, which doesn't allow a great deal of space for the larger cruise ships as they enter the port of Lisbon.

Built by the 'American Bridge Company', the bridge was opened on 6th August 1966. Due to its colouring, it closely resembles the 'Golden Gate Bridge' in San Francisco, which was also constructed by the same builder.

Close by the bridge stands an impressive statue – 'Christ the King' (Cristo – Rei), which was completed in 1969 and inspired by the similar statue in Rio de Janeiro, Brazil.

Lisbon is a beautiful city steeped in history with ancient buildings and amazing statues. It was a pleasant late summer day when we were there, and we fully appreciated the experience. It had crossed my mind that I might purchase a bottle of vintage Port, but when I saw the prices ranging from circa £50 up to several hundred pounds, I thought better of it!!

Our visit to Lisbon, the capitol city of Portugal, brought back memories of our first and previous visit to Portugal, which was probably twenty years prior to this one.

Pat and I went on an apartment holiday to the seaside resort of Quarteira, which was fine except for the weather. There was a constant cool breeze, and a really rough sea. Towards the middle of the week, I was relaxing on our apartment balcony in the late afternoon, when I spotted what appeared to be a tornado, several miles out to sea. There was a spout that seemed to connect with the sea, and the sky over the horizon, was very grey indeed.

When I pointed it out to Pat, she was sceptical, but shortly afterwards, I drew her attention to some local elderly gentlemen, who were stood on the promenade, and they were pointing to the impending storm.

As the twisting spout came nearer, it seemed to change direction from heading directly towards us, and it appeared to be heading towards Vilamoura and Albufeira, along the coast. In fact it touched land about four miles north of where we were staying at Quarteira, and whilst it did some structural damage, there were no injured parties involved.

As we were leaving Lisbon on board 'Ventura' Pat and I were attending the sail away party on the open sea deck, and as we approached the '25 de Abril Bridge', an entertainment officer, killed the music and shouted out "everybody duck"!! It really did seem that our tallest mast would collide with the bridge, but afterwards, we were advised that there was about 12 metres of clearance.

24

Trinity Bridge – St Petersburg.

We visited St Petersburg in Russia, in 2012, and took an excursion on each of our two day visit to this historic city, thereby crossing many interesting bridges. Trinity Bridge is the second longest bridge in St Petersburg and one of the most picturesque. It was constructed in 1903 and since then, it has undergone several modifications, the most recent being in 1967. It now comprises a total of 9 spans, made up of three constructed from granite, and five fixed steel arches, plus a single lift bascule section. The photograph shows the bascule open to allow traffic on the River Neva to pass through.

The bridge is 24 metres wide and supports four highway lanes of traffic, across a total length of 582 metres.

This is a most ornate bridge, built in the French Nouveau style, its construction is made up from granite, steel and cast iron. There are Globed lamps across the bridge, in groups of three, supported by cast iron brackets, and mounted on pylons. They have different coloured lights, making a splendid sight during the hours of darkness.

One of our photo stops during our first excursion was to view an historic museum ship moored in the Boishaya Nevka River, very close to the Sampsonievky Bridge. In this shot of the stern of the Russian Navy Battle Cruiser, 'Aurora', you can just see a single arch of the Sampsonievsky Bridge.

Time did not permit us to board 'Aurora' but it was still a pleasure just to view her from the embankment.

This photograph shows the ships funnels and some of her many armaments.

Despite being a museum ship, 'Aurora' has never been decommissioned and is therefore; still part of the Russian Navy, with a crew on board, headed by a 1st rank captain. She has undergone major refurbishment and is fully maintained by sea cadets from the Russian Navy.

'Aurora' was involved in numerous naval battles including the 'The Battle of Tsushima' in 1905, during the Russian – Japanese War. She was also involved in the 'Dogger Bank Incident' in 1904, when the Russian Baltic Fleet opened fire on some Hull Fishing Trawlers, mistaking them for Japanese War Ships.

Her firing of a blank shell on 25th October 1917 was to signal the attack of the Winter Palace, which formed part of the 1917 Russian Revolution, during which, the tsarist regime, was ended, and the Soviet Union was established.

I have written more extensively about our trip to St Petersburg in my book entitled 'This is the Life', which also included a visit to 'Catherine's Palace'.

25

North American Bridges

The bridges featured here, represent a wonderful holiday, comprising a 25 – night cruise with P&O, beginning and ending in Southampton, England, with four ports of call in the USA and four more in Canada.

New York City – 10th & 11th September 2013.

Following six days at sea, crossing the North Atlantic Ocean on board the cruise ship 'Aurora' we arrived at our first destination, New York City, more commonly known as 'The Big Apple'.

As we made our approach to our berth on Manhattan Island, we passed beneath the 'Verrazano Narrows Bridge'.

This is a double decked suspension bridge, which connects the Burrows/Buroughs of 'Staten Island' and Brooklyn. As we approached the bridge, the ships navigation officer informed us that Aurora's mast would clear the underside of the bridge by just 12 feet. I stood at the stern of the ship and it looked as if we were going to crash into the lower deck and you could hear passengers gasp in amazement as we cleared beneath this very large structure.

The 'Verrazano Narrows Bridge' has a central span of 4,260 feet and it was completed in 1964.

The clearance below the bridge at mean tide is 69.5 metres, which makes it a little tricky for some of the large ships to pass beneath safely.

I took the photograph from 'Aurora's' stern, shortly after we sailed beneath this magnificent looking structure.

Leaving Verrazano behind us, we could see Manhattan Island ahead with the 'Statue of Liberty' appearing on our port side. This is a splendid sight, which we have all seen pictures of before, but there's nothing like viewing it for real.

To the right of Manhattan Island we could just make out Brooklyn Bridge, in the distance, with Manhattan Bridge, almost concealed behind it. I was to visit these two iconic bridges, the following day.

As Manhattan Island got closer, we could clearly see the Manhattan skyline with the newly constructed 'Freedom Tower' standing tall, plus the 'Empire State Building'.

Most of the ships passengers were on the upper deck at this time, and I could sense great excitement as we approached our berth at pier number 90. As the ship manoeuvred alongside, we had a brilliant view of the aircraft carrier USS Intrepid, which now has a permanent mooring at the adjacent pier, forming part of the 'USS Intrepid Air Space Museum'. This aircraft carrier was built during WW2 and commissioned in 1943. She saw much action during the Second World War, including 'The Battle of Leyte Gulf'. Her flight deck has numerous vintage aircraft on board, including a spectacular Lockheed SR-71 'Blackbird' which holds the record for the fastest military aircraft ever to be in service.

Parked alongside Intrepid is a British Airways Concord, which is a magnificent setting for this famous retired aircraft. Time during this trip did not permit us to visit this very interesting museum, but If I return to New York City at some later date, it will certainly be high on my 'must do list'.

It was now midday of September 10th 2013, and after lunch we were booked on an excursion to visit the highlights of 'New York City', by luxury coach.

The weather was unusually hot for the time of year, so a tour of the city by means of an air conditioned coach was the easiest way to see as much as possible.

We had an excellent tour guide who gave us lots of interesting information, including the fact that there are more than 2,000 bridges in New York City, most of which are road bridges.

The population of New York City is 8.3 million, and it appeared that many of them were out walking the streets of Manhattan!! There are 14,500 taxis operating within the five boroughs, plus 39,000 serving Police Officers.

We spent four hours visiting many of the sights, including – Central Park, Times Square, Chelsea District, Greenwich Village, China Town, Soho, plus Wall Street, Broadway, 5th Avenue & 42nd Street.

Other points of interest included, Macys Department Store, NY Stock Exchange, & St Pauls Chapel, where America's first President George Washington prayed, following his inauguration ceremony.

Our tour finished with a visit to the 'World Trade Centre', which gave us thoughtful and sombre emotions regarding the horrific events, which had occurred twelve years prior.

The newly constructed 'Freedom Tower' stands majestic in defiance of terrorism, and symbolises America's spirit of true courage in the face of adversity.

I must admit that I thought the original 'World Trade Centre' comprised just the twin towers that came down following the terrorist attacks. In reality, there were a total of seven buildings, and the remaining five were severely damaged during the attacks, such that they had to be completely demolished.

The new site will comprise five buildings, two including the 'Freedom Tower' have been topped out, and the remaining buildings, are scheduled to be completed before 2020.

We hadn't realised that in order to visit the actual 'Ground Zero' site, you are required to have a visitors pass, which are issued free of charge, and available online.

We were disappointed that our tour operator had not arranged for these passes, therefore we were unable to visit the memorial centre. Following some discussion between our tour guide and the coach driver, we were taken to the nearby 'World Finance Centre', from where we could access an internal bridge, which overlooks the 'World Trade Centre' memorial site.

There are two 30 feet deep water features constructed within the actual foot prints of the Twin Towers. These were concealed by trees, but at least we were able to view the overall area, which includes the construction of a museum, due to open in 2014.

The new tower is an amazing sight, which brings fresh hope to the area and represents a memorial to all those who perished during the terrible events of September 11th 2001.

We all saw the devastation that the collapse of the towers made, and I find it incredible that after just twelve years, so much progress by way of repairs and reconstruction has been achieved. The new 'Freedom Tower', standing 1,766 feet tall, looks amazing, particularly so, as the bright sunshine reflects off its glass exterior.

Following this incredible tour and after dinner on board 'Aurora' we visited the sun deck from where we had an amazing view of the Manhattan skyline by night. The views were unbelievable and Pat remarked that it looked like an illuminated 'Lego Land', almost unreal, and the sight fair took our breath away.

Across the Hudson River, we could see the illuminated skyline of New Jersey, and it was pointed out to us that this was the approximate location where US Airways flight 1549 made a successful emergency landing in the Hudson River on January 15th 2009.

Also close by is the pier where the 'Titanic' was scheduled to berth in December 1912, and this has now been converted into a sports complex, which includes ice skating and many other sporting facilities.

I was amazed at how few cruise ships were present during our visit, in fact the only other cruise ship was 'Cunard's' Queen Mary 2.

On day two in New York City, which was the 12th anniversary of the 9/11 attacks, we were booked onto another excursion, this time seeing more of the city by coach, plus a ferry trip out to the 'Statue of Liberty'. After breakfast, we walked around the open deck 13 and it was a bright sunny morning, very similar to that dreaded day twelve years prior. It was a time for reflection, made more poignant with the 'Stars and Stripes' flag flying at half-mast on board 'Aurora'. It was a moving experience, looking skywards and trying to imagine the horrendous sight of those aircraft crashing into the Twin Towers. Our tour guide the previous day, had informed us that at the time of the disaster, she was staying at her mother's apartment in Brooklyn. She said, "News broke of a terrible accident when an aircraft crashed into one of the Twin Towers." She described how she visited the roof of her mother's apartment block, from where she could see the towers. She then saw another aircraft crash into the second tower, and then realised that this was no accident, and something much more sinister.

Shortly after 08-00 am our captain made an announcement that there was going to be a four minute silence to pay our respects to all the 3,000 people who lost their lives as a result of the terrorist attacks.

The period of silence started at 08-46 am, by the sounding of the ships bell, and ended at 09-00 am, again with the sounding of the ships bell. These represented the exact times when the two aircraft collided with the towers.

Pat and I found two easy chairs in one of Aurora's lounges, where we could spend this solemn occasion. We were both grateful of the opportunity to pay our heart-felt respects for all those who lost their lives as a result of those dreadful events, twelve years before.

Our excursion ashore on day two of our visit began with another coach trip to see more important sites on Manhattan Island.

The traffic was particularly heavy, being the anniversary of the terror attacks, and the area around Ground Zero was sealed off, as the relatives of those who died, are given special privilege to attend a ceremony, where all the names of the deceased are read out.

Our driver had to work out the best routing to see more places. We passed by 'Grand Central Station' and 'The United Nations' building, before heading off for our boat trip on the Hudson River.

As we arrived at piers 16 & 17, I noticed there were two iron sailing ships moored alongside, and soon discovered that they are part of the 'South Street Seaport Museum'.

One ship is the four masted 'Peking' registered in Hamburg. She was built by Blohm & Voss, when she was laid down in 1911.

She was originally operated on the lengthy sea route between Chile and Europe by F. Laeisz Company. She stands as a fine example of that type of vessel, which visited those far-away places, which were difficult for coal powered ships to reach.

The other ship is the 'Wavertree' registered in Liverpool, and she was built in Southampton in 1885 for R.W. Leyland & Company of Liverpool.

She was one of the last sailing ships to be constructed from wrought iron, and when she first went into service, she operated between Eastern India and Glasgow, transporting cargos of jute. After two years, she served the tramp routes until she was dismasted during a severe storm off Cape Horn. Her crew managed to get her to the Falkland Islands, where she remained until she was converted to a sand barge in

Argentina in 1947. She was acquired by the museum in 1968 where she remains to this day.

Having spent a brief spell in the Merchant Navy, I couldn't help wondering what stories these two fine ships could tell. Conditions on board must have me very harsh and no doubt, sailors on these ships experienced a tough working life.

It was then time to board our catamaran ferry, the 'Zephyr', which carries a total of six hundred passengers.

As we pulled away from pier 16, I was very pleased that she first headed towards the nearby 'Brooklyn Bridge', which I wanted to include in my book. We passed beneath the bridge, which gave me an excellent opportunity to take close up photographs, as well as shots of the nearby 'Manhattan Bridge'.

We then did a 'U' turn and headed down the East Hudson River, sailing close by the 'World Trade Centre' and beyond towards the 'Statue of Liberty'. We didn't have the opportunity to set foot on Liberty Island, but the boat sailed very close by, giving us good opportunities for excellent photos. This statue is truly one of the most famous landmarks in the world, and its sheer size is not apparent until you get up close. To put some idea to the scale of this colossus, the index finger pointing out to sea is approximately 8 feet in length.

Back on board 'Aurora', the captain made an announcement that he had arranged to delay our departure time, to allow us the opportunity of seeing the laser show, which was due to take place after sunset.

As dusk was approaching and the crew were preparing to leave NYC, the captain made another announcement that the security authorities had decided to put armed guards on board 'Aurora' until we reached the open sea.

Pat and I sat at the stern of the ship as darkness began to fall, and once again we were enthralled by the lights of Manhattan, which flickered in many shades of spectacular colours.

There appeared, several heavily armed police officers patrolling the deck, and this made us aware of dangers that still exist in our modern world.

A police helicopter circled above the ship, and two police launches appeared at the end of our mooring pier. I then spotted a kayak approaching our ship, which looked somewhat ominous, and my thoughts turned to possible suicide bombers. One of the police launches sprang into action and escorted the kayak away from the ship. It was no doubt some innocent individual coming close for a good view of the ship, but it caused one or two concerns amongst on-looking passengers.

As darkness fell, we put to sea and then the laser lights appeared, which in itself, proved an emotional experience. The lasers shine vertically upwards in the profile of the Twin Towers. Apparently, they shine four miles up into the atmosphere, and are visible from a range of thirty miles. As the ship sailed by, it made us think deeply about all those innocent victims of the 9/11 attacks and our departure from NYC was a little sombre!

This had been an amazing visit, which we shall always remember. I can best describe New York as a magical city, full of life and interesting places. The streets were bustling with young people, and we could have stayed much longer, but maybe we shall return at a later date!!

The Brooklyn Bridge spans the East Hudson River, connecting the Burrows of Manhattan and Brooklyn.

The main span is 1,595.5 feet in length, and it was the first steel wire bridge of its type in the world.

It is a combined suspension

and cable stayed bridge, designed by John Augustus Roebling, opening in 1883.

Situated upstream and close by the 'Brooklyn Bridge', the 'Manhattan Bridge' was opened in 1909. It is a suspension bridge, designed by Leon Solomon Moissieff, with a main span of 1,470 feet. There are many better photographs than this, but I wanted to use this particular one, which I took myself, as it brings back clear memories of our two stay visit to New York City.

Newport, Rhode Island - 12th September 2013.

Rhode Island is the smallest state in the USA, bordered by the states of Massachusetts and Connecticut. Newport itself is situated on an island south east of Providence. It is made famous by its well preserved mansion's, where the well to do Americans had their summer retreats. Newport also has a naval history and is famous for its connection with the boating and yachting fraternity.

'Aurora' anchored in the bay and passengers were transported ashore by the ships tenders. This gave us a very close-up opportunity to see many splendid motor launches and sailing yachts lined up at their moorings.

Once ashore, we set off to find our first point of interest, which is the quaint St Mary's Church where JFK (John Fitzgerald Kennedy) married his pretty wife Jaqueline Bouvier in 1953.

We were delighted that we were able to enter the church, which is plain in architectural style, but richly adorned with beautiful stained glass windows. As you will have gathered from my earlier writing, Pat and I love to visit churches, whenever we travel, and we just enjoy sitting quietly for a few minutes, whilst we say a little prayer. There was only the two of us visiting, so I made it my business to sit in the front pew where JFK would have sat, whilst he was waiting for his beautiful wife to attend their marriage service. I now have a claim to fame that I have sat in the very same seat, where a former president of the USA had sat, sixty years prior.

We then followed our local map to visit another church, this time it was a much older place of worship, Trinity Church, built in 1724. This is a timber building with a splendid tall spire.

The layout for the congregation seating is most unusual, as the pews are partitioned off into groups. Apparently, in times gone by, regular worshipers would pay for the use of one of these private cubicles, which contributed to the church's funding.

During our visit we learnt that Queen Elizabeth 2 visited the church in 1976 and other VIP visitors include George Washington, and more recently, Prince Andrew.

We moved on to find yet another church, this time a very ornate church, 'St Pauls Methodist Church'.

Built during the late 1800s, St Pauls was the very first Methodist church in the world, to have a steeple and bell.

Not far away, we located the 'White Horse Tavern', said to be the oldest operating tavern in the country. Records show that the liquor licence was acquired in 1687. It would have been very nice to sample the beer, but it was a little too early to partake!!

The last place of interest on my list was the local synagogue. This is a fine looking building named 'The Touro Synagogue', which is the oldest surviving synagogue in North America, and it houses the oldest Torah in the United States. We were unable to access the synagogue, but there was a commemorative plaque mounted just inside the front gates, which I thought worthy of recording here.

It is a famous letter by George Washington to the Hebrew congregation in Newport, dated August 21st 1780, in which religious freedom is laid down as a basic principle of the new republic.

Gentlemen.

While I receive with much satisfaction and esteem; I rejoice in the opportunity of assuring you that I shall always retain a grateful remembrance of the cordial welcome I experienced in my visit to Newport, from all classes of citizens.

The reflection on the days of difficulty and danger which are past is rendered more sweet, from a consciousness that they are succeeded by days of uncommon prosperity and security. If we have wisdom to make the best use of the advantages with which we are now favoured, we cannot fail, under the just administration of a good government, to become a great a happy people.

The citizens of the United States of America have a right to applaud themselves for having given to mankind examples of an enlarged and liberal policy: A policy worthy of imitation. All possess alike liberty of conscience and immunities of citizenship. It is now no more that toleration is spoken of, as if it was by indulgence of one class of people, that another enjoyed the exercise of their inherent natural rights. For Happily the government of the United States, which gives to bigotry no sanction, to persecution no assistance, requires only that they who live under its protection should demean themselves as good citizens, in giving it on all occasions their effectual support.

It would be inconsistent with the frankness of my character not to avow that I am pleased with your favourable opinion of my administration, and fervent wishes for my felicity. May children of the stock of Abraham, who dwell in this land, continue to merit and enjoy good will of the other inhabitants; while everyone shall sit if safety under his own vine and fig tree, and there shall be none to make him afraid. May the father of all mercies scatter light and not darkness in our paths, and make us all in our several vocations useful in his own due time and way everlastingly happy.

G. Washington

I took the opportunity of reading this letter twice as I found its sentiments very inspiring.

We spent a most pleasant few hours strolling around Newport and then it was time to return to 'Aurora' as there is a very nice looking bridge by the harbour, which I needed to photograph.

By the time I came to photograph the bridge, a sea mist had descended, hence the poor quality of the shot.

This is the 'Claiborne Pell Newport Bridge' which opened in 1969. It is a suspension bridge with deck truss approaches. Its longest span is 1,600 feet and the clearance below at mid span is 206 feet.

The bridge was constructed by Parsons, Brickerhoff, Quade & Douglas Company, at a cost of US $54,742.000

Boston MA – 13th September 2013.

I have made numerous visits to Boston when conducting business in North America.

Boston's Logan Airport was generally my point of entry into the USA, and on several occasions, I had seen the site of the 'Boston Tea Party'. As this was Pat's first visit to the city of Boston, my intention was to visit the Tea Party location.

We hopped on board a courtesy coach from our ship's berth in Boston Docks, which dropped us off at 'Quincy Market'. From there, it was a ten minute walk to where the two replica Tea Party Ships are located at 'Griffins Warf'.

There is a bridge adjacent to the Warf; known as 'Congress Street Bridge' and it is from this location, where I have previously viewed the Tea Party Ships.

In addition to the ships, the 'Beaver' and the 'Eleanor', there is a museum, which looks very interesting. We were limited by time constraints, so we were satisfied to view the two splendid replica ships, and of course, I needed to photograph the bridge to remind us of the occasion. We were very fortunate because there were actors on board the 'Beaver', dressed in period costume and they were enacting the events of 16th December 1773, when the 'Sons of Liberty' dumped tea overboard as a protest to the amount of tax imposed on tea imports by the British Government. 'Congress Street Bridge' adjacent to the Boston Tea Party Museum and two replica ships is a bascule bridge designed by 'Strauss Bascule Bridge Company, of Chicago, Illinois.

It spans 'Fort Point Channel', and was constructed in 1930 by builder/contractor Boston Bridge Works' of Boston MA.

The entire structure is 547 feet in length and the main tilting span is 93.8 feet in length.

It is a Pony Truss Strauss Trunnion Bascule Bridge, with an overhead counterweight. As the bridge no longer lifts, the counterweight has been removed.

Congress Street Bridge – Boston MA

Plaque attached to the bridge, providing details of the builder and the date of completion.

Museum visitors are on board one of the ships, as players re-enact the event, when bales of tea were thrown overboard as a protest of taxation levels imposed by the British Government.

You can see the tea floating by the side of the ship.

123

Before making our way back to our ship, we spent some time exploring Quincy Market, where there are lots of shops and restaurants, all set out in a most pleasant commercial shopping environment.

Portland, Maine – 14th September 2013.

We arrived at Portland, the capitol city of Maine on Saturday 14th September 2013. Our research had provided details of a narrow gauge railway and a nearby railway museum, so we decided we should check this out as our first priority.

We found the beginning of the narrow gauge track and followed it a short distance, to where we located the museum. Although a relatively small museum, it contains many interesting exhibits including historic rail cars and artefacts, which provide a good flavour of the early North American Railways.

We made further enquiries, and learnt that the 2 feet wide narrow gauge track stretches one and a half miles, and terminates at the edge of a sea inlet known locally as 'Back Cove'. It was a beautiful morning, so we decided to walk the full length of the track rather than wait for a ride on the train, which operates excursions along the track, at hourly intervals, during the summer months of May until October.

The one and a half mile track runs along-side the sea front, and it provides a most scenic walk. We were lucky with the timing of our visit because on Saturdays only, they use a vintage steam locomotive to haul the old carriages. As we strolled by the engine sheds we could hear the sounds of the loco being fired up ready for action.

The museum and track belongs to the 'Maine Narrow Gauge Railroad Co & Museum', and the track had been laid upon what had originally been a standard gauge track belonging to 'The Grand Trunk Railway', which opened in the mid 1800's.

Where the narrow gauge track terminates there is a wooden Trestle Bridge, which once carried the single track of the Grand Trunk Railway across the mouth of Back Cove. The bridge has a central steel span, which is a swing bridge, used to allow the passing of marine traffic.

The bridge was severely damaged by fire in 1984 and it has been out of service, and remained in the open position ever since.

I decided to include the swing bridge as it would serve as a vivid reminder of a most pleasurable walk in the New England Fall. As we stood by the bridge, we could hear the sound of the locomotive coming along the track. The driver kept blowing the whistle and ringing the locomotives bell, which all added to the wonderful atmosphere of this splendid little railway.

By the time we returned to Portland, the train was parked alongside the museum and I had a good opportunity to take photographs and find out some details about the locomotive.

It is a 0-4-4 Forney Loco number 2780 built in 1918 at the 'Vulcan Iron Works' of Wilkes-Barre, Pennsylvania. This is a fine example of early American style of locomotive with a long boiler, a tall smoke stack, and a plough mounted at the front.

This shot was taken from the end of the narrow gauge track and shows the old steel swing bridge, stuck in the open position. The plant in the left hand background is B&M Beans, who have been processing baked beans on this site, from a brick kiln method of production since 1927. This famous company dates back considerably further, as can be seen on the group company website, B&G Foods Inc.

This had been a most memorable visit and one that both Pat and I shall always remember.

Saint John – New Brunswick, Canada – 15th September 2013.

Upon arrival, this looked a most pleasant place as our ship berthed at the modern cruise terminal on the edge of the 'Bay of Fundy'.

One of the ships excursions was a coach trip to a location up the St John River known as 'Reversing Falls Rapids'. After making some enquiries, we were advised by the tourist information department that it was too far to walk and we needed to take either a coach tour, or travel there by taxi. From our map, it didn't appear that far, so we set off on foot along with a few other like-minded 'Aurora' passengers. We made our way around the harbour, passing some very smart looking water front condominiums, and a modern shopping mall.

From the harbour, there is a red coloured tarmacadam trail leading to the 'Reversing Falls' Visitor's Centre. There was some construction work in progress, which meant us taking an unofficial detour, crossing an unfenced rail track, but we did it, and then found our way back to the purpose built trail.

You follow the banks of the St John River along this landscaped trail from where there are spectacular views over the harbour and the river itself. Although it was approaching the Canadian Fall, there were many flowers alongside the trail, including different coloured wild roses.

We could see numerous seals swimming in the harbour and there were a lot of cormorants, who seemed to be very busy around the locality.

The trail led us to a major highway, running parallel to the river so we knew which direction we should take.

This highway passes close by the 'Reversing Falls' Visitors Centre, crossing over the Saint John River via the 'Reversing Falls Bridge'. We found the final stretch of the walk tough going, as the later stage is a steep up-hill climb.

Eventually, we made it, and felt a sense of achievement in finding our own way to this very interesting and unique river phenomenon.

At the visitors centre there are look out and viewing areas, from where you can observe the 'Reversing Falls and Rapids' from high level vantage points.

Alongside the bridge there is a small outcrop of rocks that form the falls and rapids.

The Bay of Fundy has the highest tides anywhere in the world, peaking at 28.5 feet.

At low tide, there are falls over the rocks heading downstream, and at high tide, the direction of the river is reversed, thereby causing the falls and rapids to flow upstream.

The very high tides in the Bay of Fundy are caused by tidal action originating in the Southern Indian Ocean, sweeping around the Cape of Good Up, and then heading northward into the Bay of Fundy. The position of the Moon at this longitude also has an effect upon these exceptionally high tides.

It was slack tide when we were at the scene of the Reversing Falls, but after a while we could see the falls flowing downstream, as the tide began to ebb. There were numerous cormorants resting on the outcrop of rocks, some of them with their wings outstretched to dry in the autumn sunshine.

The steel arch bridge is a fine structure when viewed from the side. It carries the New Brunswick Route 100 over the St John River Gorge, and was opened to the public in 1915. It replaced an earlier suspension bridge, which had been constructed in 1853.

The current structure is a steel arch type bridge, with its abutments firmly embedded in the rock formations either side of the Saint John River Gorge.

This had been a very pleasant and interesting place to visit and a trip that I would highly recommend.

Halifax, Nova Scotia 16th September 2013.

Although this is a book about bridges, and there are several in the Halifax region, I was pre-occupied by the events of 1912 and the tragic loss of the Titanic, plus the roll that Halifax played following the disaster.

Whilst crossing the North Atlantic Ocean, our captain drew our attention to our position when we were 100 miles north from the Titanic's final resting place.

As soon as we could leave our ship in Halifax, we decided to make our way to the 'Maritime Museum of the Atlantic', where there is a specific section about the Titanic.

Moored just opposite the entrance to the museum buildings, is a fine old steam ship 'CSS Acadia' and she forms part of the museum.

I was enchanted by the sleek lines of this splendid vessel, which represents the best of British engineering and shipbuilding in days gone by. The red maple leaf on the white background of the Canadian Flag, flying on the stern of Arcadia was a most memorable sight. Unfortunately the ship was closed to visitors for some reason, so we had to be content with viewing her from all angles of her exterior.

Acadia was built by Swan Hunter, Tyne & Wear, United Kingdom, and she was launched on May 8th 1913.

She was constructed as a Hydrographical & Oceanographic Research Ship, and she was commissioned into the Canadian

Royal Navy twice, serving in both World Wars. Most of her time was spent charting the coastline of Eastern Canada plus conducting surveys of Hudson Bay.

Some of Acadia's details are as follows:-

Tonnage – 846 grt

Length – 181 feet 9 inches.

Beam – 33.5 feet.

Propulsion – single shaft, two fire tube Scotch Boilers, one triple expansion steam engine producing 1,715hp.

Operating speed - 12.5 knots.

We entered the museum and began our tour of the many exhibits on show. It was all very interesting, but Pat and I really wished to spend much of our time within the section about the Titanic.

Although there were plenty of photographs and lots of interesting written information, there are surprisingly few recovered artefacts from the wreck itself. There is a wooden cabinet, a wooden deck lounger and most poignant of all, are a pair of kiddie's leather shoes, plus a ladies leather glove.

Reading the stories and viewing the exhibits, reinforced the enormity of the disaster, and it made our minds wonder what dreadful ends, many of Titanic's passengers had to endure.

After Titanic went down, several ships were chartered by the 'White Star Line' to recover as many dead bodies as was possible.

Ships including the 'Mackay-Bennet', The 'Minia', The 'Mont Magny' & the 'Algerine, all put to sea from Halifax to perform the gruesome recovery operation.

Many of the bodies pulled from the Atlantic Ocean were so badly disfigured that it would have been impossible for them to be properly identified; therefore many were buried at sea.

Those transported back to Halifax, were buried locally, but still there were many whose true identity could not be confirmed.

There is no doubt that the sinking of the 'Titanic' was one of the world's worst tragedies at sea, and it is made worse by the fact that many more lives could have been saved, had the actions of the nearby ship, the SS Californian, been different.

Pat and I visited this museum mainly out of interest regarding the 'Titanic', and we had not been aware of another disaster involving Halifax, which had caused a much greater loss of human life.

On 6th December 1917, a French cargo ship, the 'Mont-Blanc', which was fully loaded with wartime munitions, collided with a Norwegian ship, the 'SS IMO' in the 'Narrows' and shortly afterwards, there was a huge explosion, which caused sheer devastation within the nearby area of Richmond, Halifax NS.

Approximately 2,000 people were killed by the results of the explosion, with more than another 8,000 individuals being seriously injured.

Following our memorable visit to the 'Museum of the Atlantic' we spent the remainder of our time in Halifax exploring the waterfront, including the area of historic properties.

As we made our way back towards the cruise ship terminal, we came across a large statue of Samuel Cunard, the founder of the famous 'Cunard Shipping Line'. I hadn't realised that he was a native of Halifax, Nova Scotia.

There is a plaque alongside the statue from where I recorded the following details:-

Samuel Cunard

Born in Halifax NS on November 21ˢᵗ 1787, he became the eldest of Abraham & Margaret Cunard, who emigrated from Philadelphia to Nova Scotia in 1783.

His marriage to Susan Duffus produced nine children, all born in Halifax.

For more than half a century, the S Cunard & Company wharves on the Halifax waterfront were the centre of a vast shipping empire engaged in the West Indies trade.

Samuel Cunard became the foremost entrepreneur in Halifax and one of the largest owners of sailing vessels in the Maritime Provinces. He was a visionary who foresaw steam power replacing sail on the North Atlantic. He became the pioneer of ocean steam navigation when the paddle steamer 'Britannia', first flag ship of the British & North American Royal Mail Packet Company, later known as the 'Cunard Line' arrived in Halifax on its maiden voyage from Liverpool, England on July 17ᵗʰ 1840.

The advent of steam on the North Atlantic forever altered commerce and communication between the old and new worlds.

Samuel Cunard, the 'Steam Lion', Nova Scotia founder of the 'Cunard Line' was knighted by Queen Victoria in 1859. He died in London, England on April 28ᵗʰ 1865.

We concluded that Halifax is a most interesting place, combining a new modern city with much history, which we greatly appreciated. Although I was aware of a nice bridge 'The Macdonald' Bridge not far away, we had focused our attention to the waterfront region and therefore, we didn't visit a single bridge to feature in this book, but our other attractions were worthy alternatives.

Quebec City – 18th September 2013.

Following a sea day, on our journey from Halifax NS, we arrived in Quebec City around lunchtime on Wednesday 18th September. We had spent much of the morning on the promenade deck as 'Aurora' navigated the St Lawrence Sea-Way, and finally the St Lawrence River, to our berth close to the city centre. The last few miles before arriving in Quebec City are most picturesque, and we appreciated every minute.

We were scheduled to stay overnight, departing the following evening, so we needed to plan how we would allocate and apportion our time to best advantage.

In advance of our visit, my research had led me to a large cantilever bridge, upriver from Quebec City, so we decided we would make a visit to this bridge, our first priority.

After lunch, we left the ship and began walking alongside the St Lawrence River, in the direction of the bridge. We made enquiries and we were informed that it was about three miles, so as it was a most pleasant afternoon, we decided we would manage a brisk stroll to the bridge and back before nightfall.

Once clear of the urban centre, we came across a trail by the river edge, taking us in the right direction. After about a mile we came to where the Cunard, 'Queen Mary 2' was moored in the river. She was an impressive sight, berthed in this very rural setting alongside a lightly wooded area in the outskirts of Quebec City.

We kept going, but there was no sign of the bridge, so we made further enquiries. Our hearts sank just a little, when a lady cyclist told us the bridge was at least another 4.5 kilometres upriver. I was getting a little tired and concerned that if we continued much further, we may not get back to the ship before it was dark. Pat insisted that we carry on, and up ahead, we could see a church steeple. We agreed that we would continue as far as the church, and then if the bridge was still not in sight, we would begin our long trek back to the ship.

As we approached the church there was a bend in the river and shortly beyond the headland, the bridge came into view. I took several photographs of this magnificent structure and then it was time to head back.

I estimated we had covered about 12 miles in order to see and photograph 'Quebec Bridge', but in the end it was all worthwhile and an experience we shall never forget.

This huge steel structure was opened on December 3rd 1919. It is riveted steel truss structure of a cantilever design, with a 195 metre central span. The total length of the bridge is 987 metres, and it is 29 metres wide.

The Quebec Bridge is still the longest cantilever bridge in the world. It spans the Saint Lawrence River and carries three highway lanes, plus a railroad track, and a pedestrian walkway.

Its construction was blighted by disaster on two separate occasions, firstly on August 29th 1907, when part of the bridge collapsed whilst under construction, and 75 workers lost their lives.

Design changes took place, but there was a second disaster on 11th September 1916, when the central section was being hauled into position. Things went badly wrong and the central span fell into the river with the loss of a further 13 lives.

In the photograph, there is another bridge just 200 metres up river. This is the 'Pierre Laporte Bridge' which opened in 1969. It is a suspension bridge, 1,041 metres long, with a longest span of 667.5 metres. This bridge carries six highway lanes of AutoRoute 72.

Day two of our visit to Quebec City was spent exploring the city area, which was most pleasant, although somewhat tiring due to the hilly terrain. The architectural design is very French style, and the landscape is dominated by the 'Chateau de Frontenac' which towers above the Saint Lawrence River, hundreds of feet below.

We took our time and made the trek to the highest point on foot, stopping occasionally to regain our breath, and to take in the magnificent views.

At the highest point there are the ramparts and defence installations, all constructed to defend the City from foreign invaders.

As we started our descent, we stopped off to visit three churches.

The first one we entered was the 'Notre-Dame de Québec' Basilica-Cathedral. This is a very ornate church with a spectacular baldachin, which fair takes your breath away. Originally built on this site in 1647, this church was ravaged by fire twice throughout the centuries, but each time, it was rebuilt on its original foundations.

We then entered another nearby church, this time, 'Le Sanctuaire de Notre-Dame du Sacré-Coeur. Constructed in 1909 & 1910, The Shrine of Our Lady of the Sacred Heart was built by F. X. Berlinguet and Alphonse Laberge. Whilst not as ornate as the previous church, this felt a very nice place to be, and it served perfectly for our morning prayer.

The third church we visited in Quebec City was somewhat plain by comparison, namely, 'Chalmer-Wesley United Church'.

The church contains some splendid stain glass windows, which were highlighted by the strong exterior sunshine.

There was a single guitarist playing, and this gave the place a strong sense of spirituality and peace.

Whilst visiting this amazing city, my thoughts kept returning to the 'Foryd Bridge', featured earlier in this book, and the wreck of the 'City of Ottawa' which lies alongside the bridge. This early sailing ship had begun its life in Quebec City, when it was constructed by the 'Jean-Elie Gingras' Shipyard. I find it incredible that such a small ship could have sailed the oceans of the world and then flounder in the waters off North Wales in the United Kingdom.

I would have liked more time to research the location of the shipyard where the 'City of Ottawa' was built, but unfortunately time did not permit.

Charlottetown, Prince Edward Island. – Saturday 21ˢᵗ September 2013.

Following our departure from Quebec City, we had one more sea day before arriving at our last port of call, Charlottetown, in 'Prince Edward Island'.

We had nothing planned for Charlottetown, just to wander around and appreciate the pleasant surroundings on this very nice autumnal day.

Our first point of interest was a visit to St Dunstan's Basilica situated only a short walk from the cruise terminal. This is a splendid church with a spectacular circular stain glass window, positioned high above the very ornate alter.

We made our way through a marina and discovered a military museum. Unfortunately, it was closed, presumably for the weekend, but to our great surprise there was a Sherman Tank positioned outside. This fine exhibit was of particular interest to us as Pat's late father, Jack Beff, spent the latter part of WW2 serving as a gunner on one of these impressive military vehicles.

We didn't find much else to see, so following a good walk around the area; we made our way back to 'Aurora'.

Leaving Charlottetown in the evening, we could then look forward to six more days sailing, before we arrived back into Southampton.

25

Clumber Park Bridge - Worksop

This extremely ornate, triple arch limestone bridge is located in Clumber Park, Nottinghamshire, England.

We are very fortunate to reside just a few miles from Clumber Park, so Pat and I are regular visitors, and usually, at least twice per week, we take our exercise here, with a gentle stroll around the lake.

It generally takes us about one and a half hours to complete the 4.25 mile walk, with a couple of stops along the way, dependent upon our fitness levels on that particular day.

Some might think that this would become quite repetitive, but we just love the place, and appreciate the seasons, as we try to visit in all weathers. We usually pause as we cross over the bridge, just to take in the magnificent view down the lake towards the chapel.

Clumber Park, now owned by the 'National Trust' was once the ancestral home of the Dukes of Newcastle. I'm not going into great detail here about the park itself, as there is much information about the history, and present day facilities, available from the National Trust website. I just wished to complete my book of bridges with this very fine example of Palladian style architecture, constructed during the 1770s.

Its three almost semi-circular arches span the River Poulter as it flows through the serpentine lake that was created by the building of a dam further downstream. The dam, completed in 1774 took fifteen years to construct at a total cost of £6,612 - 8s - 9d (six thousand, six hundred and twelve pounds, eight shillings, and nine pence)

Of all the bridges in this book, I consider Clumber Park Bridge to be one of the most pleasing on the eye. It is an English Heritage Grade 2 listed building with an ID ref 241357. I particularly appreciate the balustrade tops, which sit upon a dentilled cornice. In my estimation, the aesthetic lines of the bridge are as near perfect as they could possibly be. The straight sloping balustrades over the bridge blend with the geometry of the three arches, to create an overall architectural structure of immense character. At each end of the bridge, the balustrades have a short horizontal section, before a continuation of the straight slope, which curve outwards, effectively widening both approaches to the bridge. The balustrades terminate, either side the bridge, with a domed topped, circular pillar approximately 32 inch in diameter.

About one hundred yards from the bridge, there is a weir of approximately four feet, created to provide a fall, sufficient to power a small water turbine.

I find it a little ironic that I included a turbine associated with my first bridge in this book, and now I can describe yet another Gilbert Gilkes & Gordon Ltd turbine, which is in close proximity to my last bridge.

This little turbine was installed to pump water from an artesian well, to the house, via an underground reservoir. It is still in situ alongside the lake in a stone built grotto. Although it's no longer in use, it remains in working order, mechanically coupled to drive a three throw ram pump.

Manufactured by Gilbert Gilkes & Gordon Ltd, the turbine was supplied to 'London Fort George & Co Ltd' (Clumber & Worksop) in 1934, who were the land owners at that time.

It is an 18 inch, series 'R', 'Francis' turbine serial number 4021, and it is capable of generating 3kw of energy, from a volume of water (11 cubic feet/sec) falling a height of 4 feet.

This is another shot of the bridge, taken on 2nd August 2013. I often stand at this location, and appreciate the splendid design and geometric lines of the structure that blend in superbly well with its surroundings. In certain daylight conditions, there is often a splendid view from this spot, when a reflection of the bridge on the surface of the water, make the arches appear as full circles.

Pat and I appreciate the wild life that is in abundance within Clumber Park. We particularly enjoy the spring when water birds are nesting, and then we can't wait for the newly hatched ducklings, goslings, signets, plus many other species of water bird fledglings, to appear.

There are numerous types of ducks including Mallards, and the little Tufted Duck, which is renowned for its diving capabilities. Occasionally, we spot a Mandarin Duck, with its fine array of exotic plumage. There appears to be an increasing colony of cormorants that are no doubt there for the fish.

In the winter, Pat takes with her a pocket full of monkey nuts still in their shells, which go down a treat with the many grey squirrels, found in one particular area of the park.

There are some magnificent trees within the park, not only indigenous species, but very large and mature, North America exotic trees, which were introduced by the second Duke of Newcastle in the late 1700s.

I don't think we shall ever tire of our walks in Clumber Park, as for us, it is a very special place, and I'm very pleased to close my book about bridges, with this one so very close to our home.

List of images

Page 6 - Penn Bridge, Bosley – Photograph courtesy of East Cheshire East Council Highways Department.

Pages 10, 12, & 13 - Macclesfield Canal Bridges – black and white adaptation of original photographs, plus front cover photograph, courtesy of author David Kitching.

Page 15 - Foryd Bridge Rhyl – black and white adaptation of original photograph, courtesy of author Peter J. Robinson.

Page 18 - Conwy Suspension Bridge – black and white adaptation of original photograph, courtesy of author Peter Lewis. Wikimedia Commons File: Three bridges across the river Conwy.jpg.
Source:http://commons.wikimedia.org/wiki/File:Three_bridges_across_the_river_Conwy.jpg?uselang=en-gb
License: This photograph is now released into the public domain by its author Peterlewis.

Page 21 - Duke Street Bridge, Birkenhead – black and white adaptation of original photograph, courtesy of author George Robinson.
Geograph.org.uk File: SJ3190: Duke Street Bridge.
Source: http://www.geograph.org.uk/photo/588922
Licence: http://creativecommons.org/licenses/by-sa/2.0/

Page 35 - Assistant Engineering Officer Chris Pownall, with mother Lucy Amelia Pownall - author Chris R. Pownall.

Page 35 – SS. Talthybius 1944 – 1971 - author Chris R. Pownall.

Page 36 - Iron Bridge Shropshire – black and white adaptation of original photograph, courtesy of user Jasonjsmith - Wikimedia Commons File: Ironbridge 002.JPG.

Page 39 - Tower Bridge London – black and white adaptation of original photograph, courtesy of author Diliff (David Iliff).
Wikimedia Commons File: Tower Bridge London Feb 2006.jpg.

Page 40 - HMS Belfast moored in the River Thames close to Tower Bridge – black and white adaptation of original photograph, courtesy of author John Goldsmith.
Wikimedia Commons File: River Thames, HMS Belfast, and Tower Bridge- geograh.org.uk – 991778jpg

Page 41 – Qasr al-Nil Bridge, taken from 6th October Bridge, Cairo - author Chris R. Pownall.

Page 43 – Chris & Pat Pownall in front of the Sphinx with the Great Giza Pyramid in the background - author Chris R. Pownall.

Page 44 – Qasr al-Nil Bridge – black and white adaptation of original photograph, courtesy of author Kristoferb.
Wikimedia Commons File: Qasr al-Nil Bridge.jpg
Arribution: - Kristoferb at en. Wikipedia
Source: ghttp://commons.wikimedia.org/wiki/File:Qasr_al-Nil_Bridge.jp
License: http://creativecommons.org/licenses/by-sa/3.0/deed.en

Page 44 – 6th October Bridge – black and white adaptation of original photograph, courtesy of author flyvancity from New York USA.
Wikimedia Commons File: 2010 Cairo 4508880334.jpg
Source:http://commons.wikimedia.org/wiki/File:2010_Cairo_4508880334.jpg?uselang=en-gb
License: http://creativecommons.org/licenses/by-sa/2.0/deed.en

Page 50 - Seven Mile Bridge, Florida – black and white adaptation of original photograph, courtesy of US Department of Transportation, Federal Highway Administration - photograph 76775, public domain.

Page 50 - Sunshine Skyway Bridge, Florida – black and white adaptation of original photograph, courtesy of Pinellas County, Florida, USA

Page 51 - Forth Rail Bridge from Dalgety Bay – black and white adaptation of original photograph, courtesy of author Euchiasmus.
Wikipedia Commons File: Forth Bridge from Dalgety Bay.jpg
Source:http://commons.wikimedia.org/wiki/File:ForthBridgeFromDalgetyBay.jpg?uselang=en-gb
License: This photograph is now released into the public domain by its author Euchiamus.

Page 53 - Royal Yacht Britannia – black and white adaptation of original photograph, courtesy of author Steve Daniels.
Wikimedia Commons File: The Royal Yacht Britannia in Portsmouth - geograp.org.uk – 1702549.jpg

Page 54 - The Humber Bridge – black and white adaptation of original photograph, courtesy of author Adamjennison111.
Wikimedia Commons File: Humber Bridge South Bank2.jpg

Page 57 - Royal Border Bridge – black and white adaptation of original photograph, courtesy of user: Ultra7
Wikimedia Commons File: 60163 Tornado 7 March 2009 Berwick.jpg

Pages 61 & 62 - Cross Keys Bridge – photographs courtesy of 'Bridge Watch'.

Page 63 - Makaranga Japanese Garden Bridge – black and white adaptation of original photograph, courtesy of authors – Mr Chick and Mrs Danna Flack – Makaranga Lodge Hotel, Kloof, South Africa.

Pages 70 & 71 - Nanpu Bridge, Shanghai – black and white adaptations of original photographs, courtesy of Leong Long, China Highlights Travel Company.

Page 78 - Bandra-Worli Sea Link – black and white adaptation of original photograph, courtesy of PDPics.com Public Domain Pictures.
Source: http://www.pdpics.com/photo/6439-bandra-worli-sea-link-mumbai/

Page 83 - Jozef Pilsudski Bridge – black and white adaptation of original photograph, courtesy of author Luke_33
Wikimedia Commons File: Pilsudski Bridge Krakow.jpg
Source:http://commons.wikimedia.org/wiki/File:Pilsudski_Bridge_Krakow.jpg?uselang=en-gb
License: http://creativecommons.org/licenses/by/2.5/pl/deed.en

Page 87 - Charles Bridge, Prague – black and white adaptation of original photograph, courtesy of author Karelj.
Wikimedia Commons File: Karluv Most a balon 2. Jpg.
Source:http://commons.wikimedia.org/wiki/File:Karl%C5%AFv_most_a_balon.jpg?uselang=en-gb
License: This photograph is now released into the public domain by its author Karelj.

Page 91 - Incheon Bridge, South Korea – black and white adaptation of original photograph, courtesy of author Jingo Jung.
Wikimedia Commons File: Incheon Bridge (7).jpg
Source:http://commons.wikimedia.org/wiki/File:Incheon_bridge_(7).jpg?uselang=en-gb
Licence: http://creativecommons.org/licenses/by-sa/2.0/deed.en

Pages 94, 95 & 96 - Sydney Harbour Bridge - author Chris R. Pownall.

Page 97 - Photograph of Blue Funnel Ship 'Hector' sailing under Sydney Harbour Bridge taken from an old post card, now believed to be in the public domain.

Page 98 – Blue Funnel Ship 'Hector' in Elderslie Dry Dock 1967 - author Chris R. Pownall.

Page 100 - Bridge of Sighs - author Chris R. Pownall.

Page 102 - Photograph of the Öresund Bridge – black and white adaptation of original photograph, courtesy of author zh:user:Mywood
Creative Commons File: Oresund Bridge from Malmo.JPG
Source:http://commons.wikimedia.org/wiki/File:Oresund_Bridge_from_Malmo.J PG?uselang=en-gb
License: This photograph is now released into the public domain by its author zh:user:Mywood

Page 104 - The 25 de Abril Bridge – black and white adaptation of original photograph, courtesy of author Jolly Janner.
Wikimedia Creative Commons. File: MSC Splendida passes under 25 de Abril Bridge.JPG.
Source:http://commons.wikimedia.org/wiki/File:MSC_Splendida_passes_under_ 25_de_Abril_Bridge.JPG?uselang=en-gb
Licence: This photograph is now released into the public domain by its author Jolly janner.

Page 107 - Trinity Bridge, St Petersburg – black and white adaptation of original photograph, courtesy of author Horvat. Wikimedia Commons File: Bridge Neva Petersburg.jpg.
Source:http://commons.wikimedia.org/wiki/File:Bridge_Neva_Petersburg.jpg
License: This photograph is now released into the public domain by its author Horvat.

Page 108 - Aurora Battle Cruiser - author Chris R. Pownall.

Pages – 110, 117, 118, 121, 123, 125, 127 & 133 - North America Bridges - author Chris R. Pownall.

Page – 123 – Boston Tea Party - author Chris R. Pownall.

Page – 128 – CSS Acadia - author Chris R. Pownall.

Page – 133 – Quebec Bridge – author Chris R. Pownall.

Pages 137 & 139 - Clumber Park Bridge - author Chris R. Pownall.

Printed in Great Britain
by Amazon